The SOCIAL SECURITY PRIMER

The SOCIAL SECURITY PRIMER

What Every Citizen Should Know

Wallace C. Peterson

M.E. Sharpe
Armonk, New York
London, England

Library of Congress Cataloging-in-Publication Data

Peterson, Wallace C.
The Social Security primer : what every citizen should know /
Wallace C. Peterson.
p. cm.
Includes bibliographical references and index.
ISBN 0-7656-0373-X (hardcover : alk. paper)
1. Social security—United States. I. Title.
HD7125.P434 1999
368.4'3'00973—dc21 99-14346
CIP

Printed in the United States of America

The paper used in this publication meets the minimum requirements of
American National Standard for Information Sciences—
Permanence of Paper for Printed Library Materials,
ANSI Z 39.48-1984.

BM (c) 10 9 8 7 6 5 4 3 2 1

To the Memory of

Eunice Vivian Peterson

Bonnie Belle Peterson

Contents

List of Tables and Figures

Tables

Figure

Preface

Social Security is the nation's oldest and most successful social program. It was introduced by Franklin D. Roosevelt's "New Deal" during the depths of the Great Depression, and millions of Americans now depend on it for retirement income, disability help, and medical assistance. There is hardly a person in the nation whose life is not touched by Social Security in one way or another.

We are living in a time when there also exists much skepticism about our government in Washington. Gone are the heady days of the past when Americans looked to the nation's capital for the solution of almost any major problem. The government that not only led this nation to victory in two world wars and guided the country through the most devastating economic depression in our history is now seen by many citizens as inept, inefficient, and all too often wholly under the sway of powerful and corrupt special interests.

The great exception to this has been Social Security. Day after day, month after month, year after year, the system works smoothly, mailing out checks to millions of citizens, untouched by the scandals that beset other parts of the government in recent years. Politically, the Social Security System has become a "sacred cow," now praised by all politicians, and virtually immune from political attack. Even Ronald Reagan, who began his political career believing that the system should be made private and voluntary, ended his career singing its praises.

Today, though, all this is no longer true. The system is in trouble, not because it is racked by scandal or because the checks are not being mailed. The trouble lies in the future, as millions of Americans fear that somehow, in some way, the system is going broke. Among young people the belief is common that when the time comes for them to retire sometime in the next century, the money simply won't be there. The hordes of baby boomers now in the workforce add to these fears. Like a pig in a python, the boomers represent a huge bulge in the nation's population profile, certain to put a strain on the system when they begin to enter the ranks of the retired in the twenty-first century.

Worries about the future of the system were compounded in late 1989 when New York Senator Daniel Patrick Moynihan tossed out a political bombshell with his suggestion that the payroll tax that bankrolls Social Security be scaled back. His proposal, coupled with angry arguments about Social Security's "Trust Funds—their uses and misuses," touched off a major debate about the nature, safety, and future of the system. This debate is destined to continue well into the future. There is irony here, for at the start of the 1980s it was believed that a bipartisan commission headed by Alan Greenspan, now chairman of the Federal Reserve System, set the direction for congressional action that fixed the system for a long time to come. What was then fixed seems to be unraveling.

It is the purpose of this book to deal with and explain these matters as clearly, precisely, and accurately as possible. This is not a long academic treatise on Social Security. The book's aim is to make understandable for the busy and concerned citizen how the system really works; what is the nature of the current "crisis," if any; and what needs to be done. The emphasis is upon the nuts and bolts of the system, what it means to you the reader today, and what it is going to mean when you retire. The bottom-line question this book seeks to answer is "Will Social Security be there when you need it?"

The book is organized into five chapters. Chapter 1, "Social Security: Is It an Endangered Species?" discusses the fears that exist for the future of the system, including a look at the baby boomers—who they are, their numbers, and their perceptions of the system.

Chapter 2, "Getting from Here to There," provides a brief history of the origins of Social Security and its evolution to the present. Chapter 3, "Things Are Not What They Seem: How Social Security Works," analyzes misconceptions about the system; its actual works, including an explanation of the trust funds and their role in the system; and the feared crisis. Chapter 4, "Social Security and the Copernican Question," suggests that we look at the problem from an entirely different perspective, one that challenges some of the assumptions which underlie current analyses of Social Security, including those developed by the trustees of the system. Chapter 5, "How to Save Social Security," offers solutions to the problems of the system, including analysis and comment upon the political action needed.

The SOCIAL SECURITY PRIMER

1

Social Security: Is It an Endangered Species?

The belief that the future of Social Security is gravely threatened is rooted in a demographic fact—the enormous bulge in the nation's population represented by the baby-boomer generation—and the fears aroused as the boomers proceed inexorably toward retirement sometime in the next century. Among the boomers themselves, many have doubts about the viability of the system, even to the point of believing that the system will be essentially bankrupt when they reach retirement. Books like *The Coming Collapse of Social Security,*[1] along with numerous articles in newspapers, the weekly newsmagazines, and other publications, add to these fears.

There is no doubt that the nation's Social Security system is facing serious problems in the not-too-distant future, but whether these problems constitute a "crisis" that threatens the viability of the system is problematical. In this chapter we shall take a thorough and critical look at all dimensions of the problem, beginning with a thorough look at the population group that is the source of the concern—the baby boomers.

The Baby Boomers

The term "baby boomers" is the popular description of the group of people, some 75 to 76 million strong, born in the twenty-year

Table 1.1

The Baby Boomers (age structure and activity by years)

Years	Ages	Activity
1945–1954	0–9 years	Infancy, grammar school
1955–1964	10–19 years	High school, college
1965–1974	20–29 years	College, marriage, family
1975–1984	30–39 years	Career, family, children
1985–1994	40–49 years	Midlife, career, family
1995–2004	50–59 years	Late career, family growth
2005–2014	60–69 years	Enter retirement
2015–2024	70–79 years	Early old age
2025–2029	80–84 years	Advanced old age

span from 1945—the end of World War II—to 1965. This cascade of babies constitutes the largest single bulge ever recorded in America's population structure. Most boomers are now approaching the 50–59–year-old age group, while the first boomers will reach retirement age around 2010, assuming 65 continues to be the standard retirement age. Table 1.1 traces that path of the boomers from birth through their retirement years, from 1945 until 2030, when most of the surviving boomers will be in their 80s. This table charts the life course of the approximately 37.5 million born in the first baby-boomer decade, 1945 through 1954. Persons born in 1954 will retire in 2019, but the last of the boomers (those born in 1964) won't enter retirement until 2029. After 2029, the retirement-age population will begin a rapid decline as the "baby-bust" population approaches retirement.

This explosion of babies took the nation by surprise, as most population experts expected that after World War II the century-long decline in America's fertility rate (births per woman) would continue. What happened, as the Population Reference Bureau, a Washington, D.C. research institution, wryly describes it, was that American couples went on a "decade-and-half-long fertility splurge."[2] From a depression low of 2.1 births per woman annually in the 1930s, the fertility rate jumped to a peak of 3.7 in 1957, falling to 3.0 by 1965, and to 1.8 by 1978.[3] The drop in the birth rate gave rise to the baby bust, which followed the baby boom. For example, in 1961, the under-5 population was 20.5 million, but by 1977 it had dropped to 15.6 million, a decline of 23.9 percent.[4]

Contrary to what many people think, the baby boom did not represent a return to the very large families characteristic of America in the nineteenth century. Rather, it resulted from a combination of earlier marriages, fewer childless and one-child marriages, and a bunching together of births. Only a minor part of the baby boom was caused by families having four or more children.

Population experts (demographers) describe blocs of children born within a certain time frame—usually ten years—as a "cohort." By identifying the baby boomers more narrowly as the cohort born between 1950 and 1959 and by comparing these numbers with the "Depression cohort" (1930–1939) and the "baby-bust cohort" (1970–1979), we get a sharper picture of the effects of the baby boom. The intermediate decades are seen as transition decades, the 1940s being the rise toward the baby boom, and the 1960s the decline to the baby bust. From this perspective, the baby-boom cohort totals 40 million, a 81.8 percent increase over the depression cohort of 22 million, while the baby-bust cohort equals 32 million, a 20 percent drop from the baby boom years.[5]

The Depression-era cohort was part of an earlier baby bust, one that saw annual births drop from an average of around 3 million from 1915 through 1929 to less than 2.4 million during the 1940s. Hard times were primarily responsible for this, although the depression years merely accelerated a drop in the fertility rate that was already under way.[6] What is more remarkable is that the parents of the baby boomers largely came from the baby bust of the Great Depression.

What caused the baby boom? Actually, nobody is quite sure,

including the population experts. Some think it was primarily an aftereffect of World War II, when millions of returning veterans were determined to pick up their lives, start families, and make a better life for their children than they had known during the depression years. This was no doubt true, aided significantly by prosperity that came with the end of the war. Most observers expected that the end of the war would bring another depression, as happened after World War I, but instead the nation entered into a long period of economic expansion and prosperity, one that carried on with only minor downturns until 1973. The GI Bill, with its aid for schooling for veterans and low-interest loans for housing, certainly contributed to marriage and family formation.

Probably of even greater significance was the cultural climate of the early postwar years. Sociologists point out that the baby boom came during a period of profoundly pro-child social values. Whether this caused the baby boom or was caused by it is uncertain, but it was a time when, as sociologist Paul Light described it, "those who didn't want children were an embarrassed and embattled minority. It was almost evidence of a physical or mental deficiency."[7] Having kids was as much a factor in the "keeping up with the Joneses" mentality as owning the right car or living in a proper house in a proper suburb. So even if the returning veterans from the war started the baby boom, social and economic conformity played a role in its continuation.

On a more theoretical level, some experts believe that the post–World War II baby boom was simply part of a more basic cycle of fertility boom and bust. According to this theory, small generations follow large generations in a predictable pattern: the basic reason being that small generations can more easily afford children than can large generations. If this theory were correct, the baby-bust generation of the 1970s would be producing a new baby boom that would be large enough to take care of their grandparents—the baby boomers—when they enter retirement between 2010 and 2030. Unfortunately, this doesn't seem to be happening. While it is true the baby boomers are having a large number of grandchildren simply because of their numbers, there has not been any upsurge in fertility rates. Currently, the fertility rate for the baby-bust cohort is barely at the replacement level (2.1 children per woman), where it is projected to remain through 2010.[8]

No sector of the nation's economy has been unaffected as the enormous baby-boom cohort moved through the economy. In the beginning, hospitals, doctors, and nurses were overwhelmed with the flood of babies that reached 4.5 million by the mid-1950s. Then came the overcrowding of primary schools and teacher shortages as the boomers reached school age. Between 1950 and 1970, the primary school-age population (5–13) grew from 32 to 37 million, a 60.8 percent increase. After the primary schools, it was the turn for high schools to feel the boomer impact. High school enrollments doubled between 1950 and 1970, while by 1963 the first of the boomers were just entering college. Most astounding of all was the percentage growth in college enrollments because of the boomers. From 1960, when there were 2.3 million Americans in the nation's colleges and universities, enrollment jumped by 213 percent to 7.2 million in 1975.[9] Because of the baby-bust generation, primary school enrollments fell by 17.2 percent between 1970 and 1985, but the number of college students continued to grow through the 1980s and 1990s. The primary reason was an increase in the proportions of high school students enrolling in college, from 23.8 percent in 1960 to 42.3 percent in 1992.[10]

By the late 1960s the boomers were moving into the young adult, marriage, and household formation state of their lives. In 1960 there were 52.8 million households in the United States. (A "household" is all persons—including adult singles—who occupy a housing unit, which is a house, an apartment, a group of rooms, or even a single room.) By 1980, the number of households had soared to 80.8 million, a 53.0 percent increase. In the 1970s alone, the prime years of household formation by the boomers, the increase in households was over 17 million. This translated into a boom in housing construction; housing starts during the 1970s were 25.7 percent higher than in the 1960s. In the 1980s and 1990s, however, housing starts fell by 15.6 and 14.0 percent, respectively.[11]

As the baby boomers matured, the nature of the American family changed drastically. To illustrate, in 1950, families made up 85.4 percent of households, and of all households, married couples accounted for 76.1 percent. But by 1993, families were only 70.7 percent of all households, and married couples had fallen to just 56.2 percent of the household total. (The term "family" refers to all persons living together who are related by birth, marriage, or adoption.) In these years, the promotion of households made up of adults living together *not* related by blood, marriage, or adoption nearly doubled, going from 14.9 percent in 1960 to 29.3 percent in 1993.[12] These figures reflect the drastically changed attitudes toward sex, marriage, and divorce that have been a part of the baby boomers' pathway through adolescence, schooling, and early adulthood.

One of the remarkable postwar achievements of the American economy was its absorption of the baby boomers into the labor force. Between 1962 and 1982, the years in which the boomers were entering into careers and work, the civilian labor force grew at an annual average rate of 2.25 percent, faster than it grew either before or after these years. In this twenty-year period, the unemployment rate averaged 6.1 percent, higher than it was in the period from the end of World War II until 1962, but lower than it has been since 1982, the year in which the last of the boomers entered the workforce. For the seventeen years from 1945 to 1982, the labor force grew at an annual average rate of 1.61 percent, and the unemployment rate averaged 4.8 percent, while from 1983 through 1996, the annual average rate of growth for the labor force was only 1.40 percent, but unemployment averaged 7.3 percent.[13] Obviously, not all boomers got what they wanted—in school, in college, in the workplace—for overcrowding and intense competitive struggle have been with them all their lives. It is a common complaint of the baby busters that all too often their own advancement is blocked by the boomers.

Ahead in less than a dozen years—2010—the first of the boomers will enter retirement, a "gray wave" that will grow in intensity until at least 2050 and possibly even longer. This surge of citizens over 65, combined with the increase in longevity for Americans, is the source of strain that Social Security faces in the coming century. In 1996 there were 34 million persons over 65 years of age in America; by 2050, according to population experts, the number of Americans over 65 will nearly double to 64 million.[14]

The most astonishing growth of all will be in the population age 85 and over, the segment of our population that requires the most extensive and costly medical care during old age. The Census Bureau estimates that eventually 1 in 4—about 18 million—baby boomers will live to be 85 or older. In contrast, in 1970, only 1 in 14 people (1.4 million) were 85 or older, in 1980, 1 in 11 (2.2 million), and in 1990, 1 in 10 (3.3 million).[15] These changes won't happen until the middle of the next century, but it is not too early for the nation to begin thinking about and preparing for these momentous population changes. We know these changes are going to happen because the people who will reach these ages are alive, and we know what the mortality rates are likely to be. What we don't know is what will happen to the fertility rates in the next century. Consequently, we don't know what proportion the elderly will be in the total population. Higher fertility rates mean a lower proportion for the elderly, while lower fertility rates will raise their proportion. If the fertility rate continues around 2.0, it will mean a smaller working population will have to shoulder a larger burden of the cost of caring for the elderly. This is the scenario that most demographers foresee.

Politically, the baby boomers are going to be the dominant voting bloc in the nation well into the next century. The first of the boomers reached voting age in 1963, and in 1992, when the nation elected Bill Clinton its first boomer president, the boomers were entering their mid-40s. The 40s are the age when about 70 percent of eligible voters of that age actually vote, a percentage that remains fairly constant thereafter. Thus, the 1990s are the time when the boomers began to have their maximum political effectiveness in terms of their proportion in the overall voting population. This is a crucial fact, for the next several years are a critical time for coping with problems in the Social Security system. The boomers not only are the population bloc who will be most affected by these problems, but they will also have to provide the energy and political will to fix them.

Attitudes Toward Social Security

Since Social Security was created in 1935, there has been support for the system, and that support has grown stronger over the years. For example, in 1936, polls showed that 68 percent of respondents supported some form of income maintenance for the aged, support that had climbed to 94 percent by 1944. Polls also show that many people have quite a good idea of how the system works. Most Americans know that Social Security benefits are financed by Social Security taxes, and that taxes on persons currently working pay for current benefits. There are still many citizens, however, who confuse the way the system works with private pension plans (see Table 1.2), a matter discussed fully in Chapter 3. Many citizens are aware that the system pays for disability as well as retirement, and that it is not a program limited to the needy.

While political support for Social Security is extremely strong—it has been called the "third rail" of American politics, "touch it and you die"—polls also show that there is increasing skepticism about the future solvency and viability of the system. In 1994, an EBRI (Employee Benefits Research Institute) and Gallup survey found that 43 percent of the respondents were not confident that Social Security would be there for their retirement. Among persons aged 18 to 34, the percentage was 52, for those in the 35-to-45 age group it was 55, but only 15 percent among those 55 years of age and older.

In a survey and summary of public opinion on the sixtieth anniversary of the system (1995), the American Association of Public Opinion found that between 1975 and 1994, the number of persons "very confident" in the future of Social Security dropped from 22 to 11 percent, while the number of persons not at all confident in the future of the system jumped from 10 to 23 percent. In 1955, another survey by *American Banker* showed that nearly one-half the people aged between 45 and 55 believed Social Security funds would be exhausted by the time they retired. Among the baby boomers, skepticism about the future of Social Security is much stronger. On the fiftieth anniversary of the system (1985), the polling organization of Yankelovich, Skelley, and White reported that 35 percent of the boomers thought that the country could no longer afford the system.[16]

Up to this point, no politician in either of our two major parties has been able to capitalize in any tangible way on these worries, especially those of the boomers. But this may change, especially as the boomers get closer to retirement. There also is a certain amount of ambivalence in these attitudes, an ambivalence reflected in both public opinion polls and focus groups that discuss the system's future. When initially surveyed, persons may not express much confidence that Social Security will be there when they retire, but in follow-up, more in-depth surveys, these same individuals almost always include Social Security as a part of their own retirement plans. Survey experts like Daniel Yankelovich say that polls reflect an immediate reaction, rather than an informed judgment. Follow-up, in-depth interviews are better at getting at the latter.

Table 1.2 summarizes the results of a poll, taken by the author, of three distinct groups: the baby boomers (33 to 53 years); the "twenty-somethings"; and persons over 54 years of age. The poll was taken in Lincoln, NE, in a upper middle-class neighborhood for the boomers and over-54 cohort, and at the University of Nebraska-Lincoln for the twenty-somethings.

These findings add both depth and detail to the foregoing comments about Social Security, but they also underscore important differences in the attitudes toward the system of the three groups surveyed—the baby boomers, the twenty-somethings, and the over-54 cohort. Of the three—and not unexpectedly—the twenty-somethings (also known as "Generation X'ers")—are the most pessimistic about the system's future, as a clear majority

Table 1.2

Attitudes Toward Social Security of Baby Boomers, Twenty-Somethings, and Persons Over 54 (in percent)

Question	Baby Boomers	Twenty-Some-things	Over 54
1. Will Social Security exist when you retire?			
Yes	83.9	44.1	100.0
No	12.9	53.9	—
2. Is there an upper limit to wages subject to Social Security?			
Yes	80.6	35.3	85.7
No	16.1	52.9	—
3. Knowledge of the upper limit.	54.8	5.9	42.9
4. Does Social Security depend on accumulation of a fund out of which benefits are paid?			
Yes	35.5	23.5	28.6
No	51.6	73.5	71.4
5. The Social Security Tax is:			
Progressive	6.5	20.6	14.3
Regressive	38.7	32.4	42.9
Proportional	54.8	35.3	42.9
6. Knowledge that Social Security was created by the Roosevelt administration.	87.1	42.1	71.4
7. Knowledge of the trust funds.			
Yes	61.3	20.6	100.0
No	38.7	76.5	—
8. Able to explain the trust funds.	41.9	2.9	28.6
9. Government should be forbidden to spend any Social Security surplus on anything other than benefits.			
Yes	64.5	41.2	42.8
No	35.5	58.8	42.8
10. Do you favor Senator Bob Kerrey's plan to invest two (2) percentage points of the current Social Security tax in private equities (stocks)?			
Yes	71.0	88.2	85.7
No	16.1	11.8	14.3
11. Should the age of eligibility for Social Security be raised to 70?			
Yes	35.5	32.4	28.6
No	64.5	61.8	71.4

12. Should an individual be free to opt out of Social Security?			
Yes	48.4	61.8	28.6
No	38.7	35.3	71.4
13. The administrative costs for Social Security are:			
Over 10 percent	64.5	47.1	28.6
Less than 2 percent	16.1	8.8	42.9
About 25 percent	19.4	38.2	28.6
14. Will the Social Security Administration collect more in 1998 in taxes than it spends for benefits?			
Yes	71.0	44.1	85.7
No	29.0	52.9	14.3
15. Social Security spending______ military spending (fill in the blank).			
exceeds	48.4	35.3	57.1
is less than	48.4	64.7	42.9

Source: Poll by author. Yes and no answers do not always add to 100 percent because some persons did not always answer individual questions.

(55.9 percent) don't expect Social Security to be there when they retire. A number of X'ers commented that the money wouldn't be there because the baby boomers would use it all!

Generally speaking, the twenty-somethings are less knowledgeable about the system than the other cohorts, as large percentages of both the boomers and over-54 cohort know that there is an upper limit to wage and salary income subject to Social Security taxes. They also have a much greater knowledge of the actual limit, something that only 5.9 percent of the Generation X cohort knows. One anomaly, though, is that a larger percentage of the twenty-somethings understand that Social Security is not like a private pension annuity—75.5 percent for the Generation X'ers compared to 51.6 percent for the baby boomers and 71.4 percent for those over 54. Given the twenty-somethings' lesser knowledge of the system, one would not have expected this. Perhaps, though, they just choose "No" when in doubt.

High percentages of the boomers (87.1) and the over-54 cohort (71.4) know Social Security was created by the Roosevelt administration in 1935, compared to only 47.1 percent of the Generation X'ers. The same is true with respect to knowledge of the Social Security "Trust Funds," as only 20.6 percent of the twenty-somethings have heard of the trust funds, as compared to 61.3 percent for the boomers and 100 percent for persons over 54. However, less than 50 percent in all three cohorts can explain how the trust funds work. A common belief is that they are individual in nature—that is, such a fund has been set up for each person paying taxes into the system.

Another rather odd finding is that two-thirds of the boomers believe that the government should be forbidden to spend any Social Security surplus on anything other than benefits, whereas almost 60 percent of the X'ers thought otherwise. A "No" answer to this question reflects a greater knowledge of the way Social Security really works, something that, in general, the boomers have in comparison with the twenty-somethings.

All three groups expressed strong support for the proposal of Senator Bob Kerrey of Nebraska to invest two (2) percentage points of the current payroll tax in equities (stocks), but strong opposition to the idea of raising the Social Security eligibility age to 70. Some even wanted to lower it! Only the X'ers voted (61.8 percent) overall in favor of allowing the individual to opt out of the system, a view that is consistent with the apparent belief of the X'ers that they are more capable than the government of looking after their retirement. Finally, of the three groups, only the over-54 cohort recognized that Social Security spending, both with and without Medicare, exceeds military spending. For Social Security alone, this has been true since 1991, and for Social Security plus Medicare it has been true since 1980.[17]

Social Security and the Economy

Before we look at the exact nature of the problem confronting the Social Security system, we need to examine the role Social Security plays in the economy. This involves the magnitude of Social Security taxes and benefits in relation to the economy overall—that is, in comparison to the nation's gross domestic product and national income—and their role in the federal budget. Economically, the effect of Social Security taxes—like all taxes—is to withdraw spending power from the economy, while the payment of benefits injects purchasing power into the economy. There are also secondary, but nonetheless important, economic effects, because Social Security taxes are levied on the working population generally, while the benefits go mostly to the over-65 population. Since the spending and saving patterns of these groups differ, changes in either Social Security spending or taxation will have different effects upon the economy.

It is important to note at this point that Social Security taxes and expenditures cannot be a part of the fiscal policy of whatever party happens to be in power in Washington. Fiscal policy involves *deliberate* changes in either taxes or federal spending to influence the overall level of taxation and spending, and, thereby, affect the economy's output and employment levels. Tax cuts, for example, may be undertaken, as the Johnson administration did in 1964, to stimulate consumer spending, thus pulling the economy out of a slump. But Social Security taxes and benefits cannot be manipulated this way, either in the short or long run, so they are not included in the arsenal of fiscal weapons at the disposal of any administration.

Table 1.3 looks at Social Security and Medicare spending in relation to the nation's GDP for the years since 1950. This gives us a good picture not only of the relative importance of Social Security spending within the context of the overall economy, but what changes have been taking place in Social Security, including Medicare, since 1950.

The major conclusion to be drawn from these data is not only that Social Security and Medicare expenditures play an increasingly important role in the economy, but that their rates of growth are, on average, nearly twice as large as the overall growth of the economy as measured by growth in the GDP. This is the aspect of the Social Security system that has especially alarmed Senator Bob Kerrey and the Bipartisan Commission on Entitlement Spending which he co-chaired. If one extrapolates

Table 1.3

Social Security and the Economy for Selected Fiscal Years: 1950–1998
(in billions of dollars and in percent)

Year	GDP	Social Security	Percent of GDP	Medicare	Percent of GDP	Combined	Percent of GDP
1950	$ 284.8	$ 0.4	0.2	—	—	$ 0.4	0.2
1955	398.0	4.4	1.1	—	—	4.4	1.1
1960	526.6	7.4	1.4	—	—	7.4	1.4
1965	719.1	17.5	2.4	—	—	17.4	2.4
1970	1,035.6	30.3	2.9	$ 6.2	0.6	36.5	3.5
1975	1,630.6	64.7	4.0	12.9	0.8	77.6	4.8
1980	2,784.2	118.5	4.3	32.1	1.2	150.6	5.4
1985	4,180.7	188.6	4.5	65.8	1.6	254.4	6.1
1990	5,743.8	248.6	4.3	98.1	1.7	346.7	6.0
1995	7,265.4	335.8	4.6	159.9	2.7	495.7	6.8
1998*	8,079.9	381.5	4.7	198.1	2.5	579.6	7.2
Average annual rate of growth (%)	7.2	13.7	—	13.2	—	14.7	—

Source: Economic Report of the President, 1969, 1997; *Current Economic Indicators*, March 1998.

*Estimated.

Social Security and Medicare expenditures far enough into the future at current growth rates, they would eventually absorb the whole of the GDP! This, of course, is an absurd outcome, but such an exercise serves to underscore the seriousness of the problem.

At this point a word is in order about the economic nature of Social Security and Medicare spending. They are what economists term "transfer spending." This is because they don't directly use up part of the GDP, but represent a portion of the national output that is literally transferred through the government by taxation to persons and families who benefit from Social Security and Medicare. As far as the latter are concerned, some of the transfer spending is received in money form as income (i.e., retirement checks) while some is received as "in-kind" services, such as the services of physicians and hospitals. Still further, some may be received in the form of food stamps, which provide the recipients with grocery store items.

Transfer spending is in contrast to the direct purchase of goods and services (i.e., the hiring of labor) by a governmental unit to do the ordinary things we associate with government—build roads and streets, run the courts and the legal system, build and operate schools, maintain armed forces, conduct foreign affairs for the nation, regulate economic activity, and many other services. The point is that for a government—any government—to do these things requires resources, which they obtain by going into the marketplace and purchasing them. The amount that governments spend for the goods and services they need represents a true measure of the part of the GDP pie that is being used for the production of government services. Since the latter are not measured by their sale in the marketplace, as is true for privately produced goods and services, the cost to governments of the resources needed to create and supply public services is the only measure we have of their value.

To illustrate the foregoing, governments at all levels in the economy—federal, state, and local—spent $2,335.1 billion in 1995, of which $1,358.3 billion was for goods and services. The latter was equal to 18.7 percent of the 1995 GDP ($7,253.8 billion). The difference between total spending and spending for goods and services was $976.6 billion, which was equal to 13.5 percent of the 1995 GDP.[18] This is the amount of the national output transferred by governments from one segment of the population to another in 1995. The most common transfers—or "entitlements" as the Kerrey Commission prefers—consist of not just Social Security and Medicare, but also spending for welfare and family assistance, unemployment compensation, veterans benefits, grants-in-aid to state and local governments, subsidies to business, and net interest on the public debt.

A fundamental question is this: what proportion—or share—of a nation's GDP can be transferred via government from producers (the working population) to nonproducers (the retired and disabled population) without an adverse impact upon incentives to produce? This is essentially a political question, but one of enormous importance. It gets to the heart of one of the most widespread criticisms of the modern welfare state, a criticism that is voiced primarily by conservatives. What lies behind the question is the fear that because Social Security benefits must ultimately be financed by taxation, at some point incentives may be affected by the level of taxes.

Has the economy reached this point? There really is no way of knowing, although there has been a decided slowdown in the rate of the economy's real growth—the GDP in constant dollars—since 1973. From 1950 through 1973, the economy grew at an annual average rate of 4.1 percent, an exceptionally robust level, but from 1974 through 1997 the growth rate dropped to an annual average level of 2.6 percent. From 1950 through 1970, a period before Medicare entered the picture, Social Security expenditures averaged 1.7 percent of the GDP. After 1970 and through 1997, Social Security plus Medicare averaged 6.1 percent of GDP, a 258.8 percent relative increase.[19] Did this cause the slower rate of GDP growth? It may have been a factor, but there were other forces at work after 1973, especially the oil crises of 1973–74 and again in 1979.

Table 1.4 presents another way of viewing Social Security and the economy, as it compares Social Security benefits and taxes to the national income. This is a useful comparison because the national income represents the money income earned by all those who supplied resources—labor, capital, and land—for producing the national output.

Like Table 1.3, the figures in this table show that both Social Security benefits and taxes are growing significantly faster than the national income, an average of 14.7 percent per year for benefits, 10.7 percent for Social Security taxes, as compared to 7.0 percent for the national income. Thus, between 1950 and 1998 Social Security benefits jumped from an average of 0.3 to 9.3 percent of the national income, while Social Security taxes rose from an average of 1.8 percent of the national income to 9.0

Table 1.4

Social Security Benefits, Taxes, and the National Income for Selected Fiscal Years: 1950–1998 (in billions of dollars and in percent)

Year	National Income	Benefits	Percent of NI	SS Taxes	Percent of NI	Income Taxes	Percent of NI
1950	$ 241.1	$ 0.8	0.3	$ 4.3	1.8	$ 15.8	6.6
1955	331.0	4.4	1.3	7.9	2.4	28.7	8.7
1960	462.2	7.4	1.7	14.7	3.4	40.7	9.5
1965	587.8	17.4	2.9	22.2	3.8	48.8	8.3
1970	836.6	36.5	4.4	44.4	5.3	90.4	10.8
1975	1,295.5	77.6	6.0	84.5	6.5	122.4	9.4
1980	2,216.1	150.6	6.8	157.8	7.1	244.1	11.0
1985	3,351.5	254.4	7.6	265.2	7.9	334.5	10.0
1990	4,652.1	346.7	7.5	380.0	8.1	466.9	10.0
1995	5,912.3	495.7	8.4	484.5	8.2	590.2	10.0
1998*	6,207.9	579.6	9.3	557.8	9.0	691.2	11.1
Average annual rate of growth (%)	7.0	14.7	—	10.7	—	8.2	—

Source: Economic Report of the President, 1968, 1997; *Current Economic Indicators*, March 1998.

*Estimated.

percent. Even more significant because of the essentially regressive nature of Social Security taxes, they jumped from being equal to just 27.2 percent of income taxes in 1950 to 80.7 percent in 1998. Clearly these changes have shifted the total tax burden increasingly onto the backs of lower-income taxpayers, as overall the progressivity of all federal taxes is undermined.

Tables 1.5 and 1.6 present yet another view of the role of Social Security in the economy, one that clearly underscores the coming crisis in the system. Table 1.5 compares projected income, outgo, and the Trust Fund balances for 1998 trough 2029, while Table 1.6 takes a very long-term view—through 2075—of the solvency of the system by comparing income and cost rates for 1998 through 2075.

Table 1.5

Projected Income and Outgo and Trust Fund Balances for OASDI and HI for Selected Fiscal Years: 1998–2029 (in billions of dollars)

Year	OASDI and HI Income	OASDI and HI Outgo	Trust Fund Balances
1998	$456.2	$377.0	$ 706.5
2000	474.3	390.9	823.5
2005	527.5	433.0	1,115.6
2010	578.7	489.0	1,378.5
2015	620.2	568.1	1,484.5
2020	642.7	665.0	1,293.5
2025	641.3	760.4	717.0
2029	635.1	835.0	—*

Source: 1997 Annual Report, Board of Trustees of the Federal Old-Age and Survivors Insurance and the Federal Disability Insurance Trust Funds, 197.

*Year of exhaustion of the Trust Funds.

These figures show that the system is clearly in good shape until 2018, which is the first year in which receipts from Social Security taxes begin to fall short of benefits paid. One might say that is the first crunch that the system will face in the next century, for at that point the Social Security Administration will have to begin cashing in some of the Treasury obligations it holds in order to finance some of the benefits being paid. At this point, though, the problem is in the lap of the Treasury, for it will have to come up with the money to redeem the obligations held by the Social Security Administration. Aside from the unthinkable proposition of simply printing the money, the Treasury can get the money from only two places—taxes or borrowing. More on this subsequently.

Here is a good place to elaborate on the Social Security trust funds, whose nature and role is not widely understood. In fact, it is a lack of understanding of the role played by the trust funds that gives rise to a complaint heard with increasing frequency these days to the effect that "they are spending our money." The "they" in this scenario are presumably the bureaucrats who run the Social Security system, and the "our money" is the excess of tax collection over benefits that now find their way into the Treasury and enter the stream of general government expenditures.

First, it is essential to understand that the trust funds, which are as old as the system itself, are primarily an accounting device. When Social Security was established by Congress and the Roosevelt administration in 1935, an immediate question was this: what should be done with the surplus tax revenues that the system would generate for several years? There would be surplus tax revenues because the Social Security taxes went into effect once the legislation was passed, but it was not until 1940 when the first benefits were paid. The first beneficiary was a Miss Ida Fuller, a retired law firm secretary, who paid into the system less than $100 in Social Security taxes, but received in benefits about $21,000 before she died in 1975.[20]

The Roosevelt administration was pressured to allow Social Security surpluses to be invested in private securities—primarily equities—but objected on the grounds that in a few years the federal government might wind up owning a large chunk of the private economy. Instead, it was decided that any Social Security surplus must be invested in a special obligation of the U.S. Treasury—that is, a bond. These Treasury obligations are special because unlike most other Treasury obligations—bills and bonds—they are not traded on the financial markets. Like other Treasury obligations, they earn interest, and are held by the Social Security administration until presented to the Treasury for payment.

So what happens to the money when there is a surplus of Social Security tax collections over Social Security benefits paid? It goes to the Treasury in exchange for the IOU given to Social Security; and like all other money received by the Treasury, whether from taxes or borrowing, it enters the income stream and is spent by the federal government for its varied activities. Since these obligations are held only by the Social Security system, the surpluses really are "earmarked" for the beneficiaries of the system, because when they are presented to the Treasury by the Social Security administration for payment, the only use that can be made for the money received is to pay benefits.

It is essential also to understand that the obligations the Social Security system gets from the Treasury are backed by the "full faith and credit of the United States government," as are all obligations of the U.S. Treasury. In the vast array of financial obligations available for investment in the American economy, no obligations are safer than those of the U.S. government.

If 2018 represents the first "crunch" facing the Social Security system, 2029 is the year when the truly big crunch hits. In this year, the Trustees of both Old Age and Survivors' Insurance (OASI) and Disability Insurance (DI) trust funds project they will be exhausted. The real crisis will develop very rapidly; in just fourteen years after 2015, when the trust funds balances are at a peak, they will be exhausted (2029). The rosy element in this scenario is that there is time—ample time for the economy to face up to the coming problem and begin to devise acceptable solutions. The first crunch is still twenty years away, and the big crunch lies thirty-one years down the road. The real problem is whether Americans can be persuaded to face in the immediate future a problem that in the minds of many is, perhaps, light-years away!

Table 1.6 contains another set of data that define the problem, showing projections from 1998 through 2075 for the balance between income and cost rates. These projections are based on the law as it exists in 1998. The income rate is the ratio of projected income from tax receipts to taxable payrolls and the cost rate is the ratio of benefit expenditures to taxable payrolls. The difference between the two is called the "actuarial balance" of the system. For the system to be in actuarial balance over this seventy-seven-year period, these two ratios would have to be equal.

These figures show in stark simplicity how the baby boomers fit into the picture and how rapidly the Social Security crunch develops once they begin to retire in 2010. Shortly after that year, the actuarial balance between income and outgo turns negative, changing from a positive value of 0.26 percent in 2010 to a staggering negative value of –6.87 percent in 2075. What this means is that the combined tax on taxable payrolls for employees and employers

Table 1.6

Projected Income and Cost Rates* for OASI and DI for Selected Years: 1998–2075 (in percent)

Year	Income Rate	Cost Rate	Balance
1998	12.63	11.61	1.02
2000	12.64	11.73	0.91
2005	12.67	11.98	0.71
2010	12.73	12.48	0.26
	Baby boomers begin to retire		
2020	12.92	15.14	–2.22
2030	13.09	17.47	–4.38
2040	13.16	17.78	–4.61
2050	13.21	17.97	–4.76
2060	13.28	18.72	–5.45
2070	13.32	19.18	–5.86
2075	13.34	19.42	–6.87

Source: 1997 Annual Report, Board of Trustees of the Federal Old-Age and Survivors Insurance and the Federal Disability Insurance Trust Funds, 1997.

*Income rate is the ratio of income from tax revenues to OASDI taxable payrolls; cost rate is the ratio of expenditures for benefits to OASDI taxable payrolls. The balance is the income rate minus the cost rate, and measures the excess of income over costs as a percent of taxable payroll.

would have to be 19.42 percent to finance OASDI spending. Thus, it would take a 67 percent increase in Social Security taxes to keep the system solvent through 2075, an increase that is clearly unrealistic politically.

There is the further complication that these figures understate the true magnitude of the problem, since they pertain only to the retirement and disability part of the Social Security system. What is not factored into the picture is Medicare, which consists of hospital insurance (HI) and supplementary medical insurance (SMI). HI is Part A of Medicare, and it is financed by a 1.45 percent tax on employees and employers on *all* payrolls. SMI is Part B of Medicare. It covers costs for physicians and outpatient, hospital, and other services for the aged and disabled, but is not financed by payroll taxes. Rather, it is financed in part by premiums charged to the beneficiaries and by general tax revenues.

In 1996, according to the Trustees of the SMI Trust Fund, premiums covered 26.7 percent of outlays for Part B of Medicare, but are expected to decline to 16.0 percent by 2006, and a progressively smaller amount in subsequent years. Like Social Security hospitalization insurance (Part A of Medicare), payments to physicians and other medical services covered by Part B are growing faster than the economy as a whole. In 1996, SMI expenditures were nearly 1 percent of the GDP; they are expected to grow to 2.5 percent by 2020 and 3.4 percent by 2075.[21]

Finally, in Table 1.7 we bring together all three major components of the American welfare state—Social Security retirement and disability benefits, hospital insurance, and supplementary medical insurance—as a projected percentage of the GDP from 1997 through 2070. This gives us the sharpest picture yet of the magnitude of the transfer problem facing the American economy in the next century. We must not lose sight of the fundamental fact that *all* benefits paid under these programs, irrespective of how they are financed, represent a transfer of a part of the nation's output from the employed or working population to those receiving the benefits. So, the ultimate political as well as economic decision bound up in the looming "crisis" for Social Security is simply this: how large a share of the nation's real output are we as a people willing to transfer to the retired, the disabled, and the over-65 sick and hospitalized part of our population?

The outlay that is projected to grow most rapidly is SMI, payments to physicians and hospitals for medical services, a not unexpected development as the nation's population ages but its life expectancy improves. Between 1997 and 2070, SMI spending is expected to increase by 277.8 percent. In the next century people will be living longer, but they also will require—and demand—more and better medical care. There is no reason to expect this to change. Hospital outlays follow with an expected 177.8 percent increase between 1997 and 2070. Old age pensions and disability benefits will grow the least; their growth

Table 1.7

Projected Spending for OASDI, HI, and SMI as a Percent of GDP: Selected Years (in percent)

Year	OASDI	HI	SMI	Total
1997	4.7	1.8	0.9	7.4
2000	4.6	1.9	1.7	7.6
2010	5.0	2.4	1.8	9.2
2020	6.3	3.2	2.5	12.0
2030	7.3	4.0	3.1	14.4
2040	7.6	4.5	3.3	15.4
2050	7.6	4.6	3.2	15.4
2060	7.8	4.7	3.3	15.8
2070	7.9	5.0	3.4	16.3
Percent change	68.1	177.8	277.8	120.3

Source: 1997 Annual Report, Board of Trustees of the Federal Old-Age and Survivors Insurance and the Federal Disability Trust Fund, and the *1997 Annual Report of the Board of Trustees of the Federal Supplementary Medical Insurance Trust Fund.*

reflects the increased proportion of the over-65 population in the nation. In 1995, persons over 65 accounted for 12.5 percent of the total population; by 1975 this percentage will reach 23.6, an 88.8 percent gain in the relative numbers of persons over 65 years in age.[22]

Some Concluding Comments

Two broad comments are in order to conclude this chapter. The first involves the assumptions that underlie the numbers contained in this chapter. These involve, first, assumptions made by the Trustees with respect to rates of growth for real GDP, wages in covered employment, the consumer price index, and the growth in the labor force, the average annual unemployment rate, and the average annual interest rate for the period 1997 through 2075. The numerical values given these assumptions are contained in Appendix 1. Second, the Trustees assume no changes in the current laws affecting Social Security and Medicare for the period under review.

The second comment is this. In the final analysis, the long-term problem facing the nation's Social Security system, including Medicare, is rooted, first, in population dynamics stemming from the baby boomers, and, second, in the economy's performance between now and 2075. The first is largely a given, about which not much can be done, for the baby boomers (and their twenty-something offsprings) are here, but the economy's performance can, within limits, be changed by appropriate public policies.

This is why the time element is so crucial. The problems confronting Social Security are real, but they are not about to come crashing down upon us. As a nation, we have the luxury of time to ponder and develop solutions for these problems. But this won't happen unless a leadership emerges that is up to the task.

— 2 —

Getting from Here to There: A Capsule History of Social Security

An appropriate place to begin this short history of Social Security is with an examination of the concept of "social insurance." Social Security is the largest element in America's system of social insurance, although in the minds of many people the two are seen as interchangeable, a view that is not quite correct.

The Nature of Social Insurance

Most of us are familiar with the various forms of private insurance, such as life, fire, theft, liability, and so on, but not all of us can define precisely the meaning of the term "insurance." Professor George E. Rejda of the University of Nebraska-Lincoln, one of the nation's foremost insurance scholars, defines insurance essentially as the pooling of risks of fortuitous—unexpected and unforeseen—losses by the transfer of those risks to a larger group, combined with compensation to the victims of a loss.[1] The most common kinds of losses insured privately are loss of income due to the loss of life (life insurance), large expenses and sometimes the loss of income due to accident or illness (health insurance), the loss of or damage to property because of fire or theft (casualty insurance), and protection against losses caused by a person's negligent behavior (liability insurance). Private insurance involves a contract between an individual—or sometimes a group of individuals, like Blue Cross and Blue Shield medical insurance—and the company that offers the protection. Private insurance is basically voluntary.

For insurance to be "social" rather than private, a number of features must be present. First, participation is mandatory or compulsory, normally specified by law. This is the situation for Social Security, even though there may be specific exemptions, as for some state and local government employees under Social Security. The mandatory feature of social insurance eliminates what insurance experts call the problem of "adverse selection." This involves the tendency of the "good risks" to opt out of any insurance programs and the "bad risks" to dominate, a condition that raises costs.

The second point follows from the foregoing, that is, it is governments that create social insurance programs, for only governments have the power to mandate participation. The actual running of the programs may be by government or it may be delegated to the private sector. Medicare is like this. It is mandated by the federal government, but private physicians and hospitals actually provide the services—that is, run the program.

A third point involves compulsory financing. Usually the resources need to run social insurance programs are obtained by taxation, most often taxes on employees and employers (payroll taxes) are used, as in America's Social Security system. This leads to a fourth feature, which is that eligibility for benefits under social insurance programs depends in part on the contributions (i.e., taxes) by the individual, the individual's employer, or both.

Finally, we should note that the benefits to be paid are prescribed by law, that they are not always directly related to the amount of contributions—Social Security benefits are determined in a manner that redistributes income toward lower-wage workers—and that the taxes that support a particular social program are explicitly earmarked to pay the benefits received under the program.

Social insurance programs as they have evolved in the United States and other industrial states rest upon a common philosophy. Although most members of society depend upon money income derived from work, by either oneself or other family members, all persons are subject to common risks that threaten the income stream—injury, illness, unemployment, death, and retirement. Since the threat to income from these risks may overwhelm the individual and the individual's family ability to cope with them, most Western nations have used the political process to "socialize" these risks. That is to say, by means of social programs such as Social Security, some or all of the threat of income loss is shifted from the individual and the family to society as a whole. Socialization of risk is the basic philosophy that underlies all social insurance programs.

We need to pay careful heed to the word usage here. We are not talking about socialism as the term is normally understood, which pertains to ownership of business and industry by the government. We are talking about a process in which certain risks are shifted from the individual and the individual's family to society as a whole. This is what to "socialize" means in this context. Thus, Social Security partly socializes the risk that an individual upon retirement will not have sufficient income.

An issue common to all social insurance programs is that of "means testing." This refers to determining whether an individual or an individual's family has a "demonstrated need" for the benefits available under the program. In a program such as Social Security, there is no means testing, the benefits are available on the basis of past work and past contributions (i.e., taxes paid), irrespective of the beneficiary's current economic situation, rich or poor. Other social insurance programs, like aid to families with dependent children—what the public generally regards as welfare—food stamps, and Medicaid, are means-tested; benefits are available only to those whose income falls below a certain level. Means-tested programs are far less popular than are programs that are universal like Social Security, in which benefits are often regarded as earned because of taxes paid during an individual's working life. Further, the non–means-tested social programs are usually cheaper to administer.

The Social Security Act of 1935

Social insurance programs in the modern sense date back to the late nineteenth century. In part this was because it was not until then that industrial nations had begun to develop enough of a surplus of production to make it possible to transfer a part of the national output to the retired population on a systematic and sustainable basis. It was also due to the fact that only then were some of the more serious social ills resulting from industrialization becoming widely apparent. Germany under the "Iron Chancellor," Otto von Bismarck, pioneered in establishing the first old-age and survivors pensions in 1889, followed by similar programs in Denmark in 1891, France in 1905, and Britain in 1908. America's entrance on this stage came far later, for it was not until the Great Depression of the 1930s that the nation began to get serious about the matter.

In the early summer of 1934, President Roosevelt established a Committee on Economic Security, chaired by Frances Perkins, at that time Secretary of Labor. The Perkins Committee completed its work late in the year, and at the beginning of 1935 Roosevelt sent its recommendations to Congress. A factor affecting the urgency with which Roosevelt approached this problem was the growing popularity of the Townsend Plan, which advocated paying every elderly citizen $200 a month. Roosevelt feared Dr. Townsend and his plan might threaten his reelection in 1936, so he wanted to have something concrete to take to the voters before then.

Aside from this concern, Roosevelt wanted two things in the system. First, it had to be differentiated from the "dole," which meant that it had to be contributory to some extent. Second, it had to be self-financing, by which Roosevelt meant that the source of finance for the system had to be identified and earmarked for the beneficiaries of the system. There are two ways for a system to be self-financing; it can be either *pay-as-you-go* or *pay-for-yourself.* In a pay-as-you-go system, current taxpayers pay the benefits received by current beneficiaries, whereas in a pay-for-yourself system each generation pays for its own benefits. It would do this by an accumulation of funds earmarked for each beneficiary, out of which benefits would be paid at retirement, for disability, or to survivors. This is analogous to private insurance, and when the fund is large enough to pay all claims, it is described as "fully funded."

As a result of the findings of the Committee on Economic Security, recommendations of the Roosevelt administration, and deliberations in Congress, the Social Security Act passed on August 14, 1935. The Social Security Act has five major titles, or in plain English, parts. Title I provided grants to the states for assistance to the aged; Title II established the Social Security system; Title III provided grants to the states for administering a system of unemployment compensation; Title IV established the Aid to Dependent Children (ADC) program; and Title V provided grants to the states for aid to the blind. Basically, the act set up a system of old-age pensions based on compulsory "contributions"—that is, a payroll tax—a system of unemployment compensation, and a structure of aid (or public assistance) to persons sometimes characterized as *the deserving poor*, namely the aged, the blind, and children.

Of the five social programs established by the 1935 legislation, only one, the Social Security system, is wholly under the control of the federal government. The other four are administered by the states, even though the bulk of the financing comes from the federal government. From the beginning, the states have determined eligibility for and the amount of public assistance, an approach that generally reflected the dominance of southerners in Congress, who feared that generous federal benefits would undercut the low wage structure in the south and threaten the black-white caste system.[2] One consequence of this has been a wide diversity between the states in the amount of unemployment compensation and public assistance benefits.

The issue of pay-as-you-go versus pay-for-yourself was settled in 1939, when the original act was amended to include benefits for survivors and Congress refrained from raising the payroll tax above the original level of 1 percent each on the employee and the employer, an action that would have been necessary to make the system a fully funded, pay-for-yourself system. In spite of this, and in part because all participants in the Social Security system have accounts that are numbered, many persons persist in believing that their benefits are—or will be—paid out of a fund accumulated by their contributions. The use of the word "contributions" to describe Social Security taxes contributes to this illusion.

Also by 1939 the mechanics for the collection of Social Security taxes and the payment of benefits were worked out, using the accounting device of a "trust fund" to do this. Money collected for Social Security was automatically placed in a trust fund, from which disbursements were made to the Treasury when benefits were to be paid. The advantage of this was that it was no longer necessary for the Social Security Administration to go to Congress for an annual appropriation of funds to meet its obligations. The trust fund accounting device is now widely used by the federal government for such varied activities as airport and highway construction, unemployment compensation, land and water conservation, and other activities in which taxes are earmarked for special purposes.

An unstated but implicit assumption of the landmark 1935 legislation was that poverty in America was primarily the result of a loss of income because of the risks inherent in an industrial society. These included unemployment, insufficient income after retirement, and income losses due to the death or disability of the family breadwinner. It was not until later during the Kennedy administration that we began to understand that the causes of poverty in modern American are far more complex.

The Social Security Act also divided the approach to income support programs (transfer spending) into two major categories, a division that has persisted ever since. The division is between Social Insurance programs and Public Assistance programs. The former includes all cash and in-kind benefits paid out through the

Old Age and Survivors and Disability Insurance (OASDI) program—what the public thinks of as Social Security—and unemployment compensation. As already pointed out, benefits under these programs are not means-tested, but are tied in to prior contributions. In contemporary usage, these benefits are often called *entitlements.* Their general objective is to keep persons and families from falling into poverty because of a loss of income due to retirement or other unexpected events, such as mass unemployment, illness, or the premature death of a family head.

Public assistance is different. Programs in this category aim at poverty and are designed to increase either the money incomes of the poor or their real incomes through in-kind benefits, such a food stamps. These programs are means-tested, and generally fit the popular conception of "welfare." No prior contributions are required for eligibility. The 1935 Act established two basic programs under this label—ADC (Aid to Dependent Children) and aid to the blind and aged. Other programs of public assistance were established subsequently.

Social Security After 1935

Social Security now is extremely popular, but it was not immediately so. In fact, for the first fifteen years of its existence, the program was in a precarious condition, being under almost constant attack by the Republicans, most of whom had opposed the act in the first place. The Social Security tax, although only 2 percent of taxable payrolls, went into effect immediately, and was, of course, quite visible. In the early years there were very few beneficiaries, so it was a long time before a strong constituency developed in support of Social Security. In the period from 1935 through 1950 more aged were helped by public assistance than by Social Security. What finally put Social Security on a secure basis were amendments adopted in 1950, following recommendations of an advisory council that issued a series of reports between April and December of 1948. The 1950 amendments expanded benefits by 77 percent; raised the combined employer-employee tax to 3 percent and the taxable wage base from \$3,000 to \$3,600; added the self-employed to the program; and developed a new schedule of future tax rates.[3]

By 1952 Republicans had largely dropped their opposition to Social Security, joining with Democrats in the bipartisan support that has made Social Security the "third rail" of American politics. In July of 1952 a 15 percent increase in benefits was passed with no hearings whatsoever in the House—this was in contrast to the year and a half it took to get the 1950 amendments passed. Next, in 1953 coverage was expanded to include farm operators, benefits were raised by another 13 percent, and the tax base was raised from \$3,600 to \$4,200. Rising real wages were one reason it was possible during these years to pass such generous increases in basic benefits. From 1940 through 1959, real wages grew by more than 2.8 percent a year, in contrast to the 1960s, when their real growth rate dropped to 1.1 percent, and the 1980s and 1990s, when the real growth rate fell to –0.8 percent per year.[4]

After 1953, the issue in Social Security coverage turned to disability insurance. Earlier, two members of the Perkins Committee on Economic Security had recommended that disability insurance be included in the Social Security package, but both Secretary Perkins and President Roosevelt believed this was too controversial an issue to be included in the report on old age assistance sent up to Congress. They wanted to get old age insurance firmly established before turning to disability and health insurance, topics even more controversial than retirement insurance.[5] Even within the Social Security administration, disability payments were controversial as compared to retirement benefits.

Nonetheless, the disability issue would not disappear. The advisory council whose recommendations were the basis for the 1950 amendments also recommended that a disability insurance program be added to Social Security, a proposal that won approval in the House in 1950, but failed to pass the Senate. Some progress was made in 1954 when the Eisenhower administration supported what became known as the "disability freeze," a proposal that preserved the benefits of a person with a disability, even though the person had dropped out of the labor force before the age of 65 because of the disability. Finally, and against the wishes of the Eisenhower administration, the Democratically controlled Congress in 1956 passed a disability insurance program, one that set up its own trust fund, which limited benefits to persons 50 years of age and older, but did not extend benefits to the dependents of persons receiving disability benefits. In 1958, Congress again modified Social Security, extending benefits to dependents, and eliminating the age-50 requirement, thus making disability insurance available to workers of all ages.

Medicare and Medicaid

For the next ten years—1956 through 1965—health care for the aged became the leading issue in the politics of Social Security. In the discussions leading up to passage of the Social Security Act in 1935, the matter of health care and health insurance was discussed, but never took the form of a concrete proposal. President Roosevelt was reportedly in favor of a system of national health insurance, although his administration did not submit a formal proposal for national health insurance to Congress. The Truman administration proposed national health legislation, but it got nowhere in Congress, especially in the face of strong opposition from the Republicans and the American Medical Association.

After Truman's unsuccessful efforts, the focus for health insurance shifted from plans aimed at the entire population, as in European countries, to a program for retired persons already receiving Social Security. In the 1960 presidential campaign, Senator John H. Kennedy made health care for the elderly a major issue, coining in the process the term "Medicare." Subsequently, the Kennedy administration gave Medicare a legislative priority, but it failed by a single vote in the Senate in 1962 to get its health care bill passed.

It was Lyndon B. Johnson's landslide victory in the 1964 presidential election that finally led to the passage of the major health care legislation we now have, namely Medicare and Medicaid. In

January 1965 the Johnson administration submitted a hospital and health care bill to Congress—Hospital Insurance, Social Security, and Public Assistance Amendments of 1965—which provided for both hospitalization and payment for all medical services, including doctor's fees, associated with hospitalization for up to sixty days.

The administration bill ran into trouble in the House of Representatives, where Wilbur Mills, Chairman of the critical Ways and Means Committee, objected to the part of the bill for the payment of doctor's fees. Instead, he proposed that the administration's version of hospitalization coverage be combined with a proposal submitted by a Republican congressman, one that required payment for part of doctor's services through premiums deducted from the Social Security checks of retired persons. A compromise was worked out in the joint Senate-House conference committee, the result of which was the passage of the Social Security Amendments of 1965 on July 28, the most far-reaching changes in Social Security since the program was created in 1935.

Medicare and Medicaid were the two major changes brought about by the 1965 legislation. Medicare set up a system of health care for persons 65 years of age and older and is technically a part of the Social Security system, while Medicaid established a program of medical care for the poor. It is a part of public assistance—or "welfare" as the public understands the term—while Medicare is classified as an entitlement.

Medicare consists of two parts. Part A is hospital insurance (HI), which covers all major inpatient hospital service, related posthospital care for the aged, home health services, and hospice care. In the case of one major illness—kidney failure and dialysis—persons are covered irrespective of age. This resulted from successful lobbying by the National Kidney Foundation, something the national organizations for heart disease and cancer were not able to accomplish. The hospital insurance portion of Medicare is financed by a payroll tax of 1.45 percent each on the employee and employer, and a 2.90 percent tax on the self-employed. Unlike OASDI (retirement), there is no upper limit to wages which are subject to the HI payroll tax. Also like OASDI, HI has its own trust fund, and all covered workers who pay OASDI taxes also pay the HI tax. As of 1998, the combined tax rate for OASDI and HI was equal to 15.3 percent.[6]

In contrast, Part B of Medicare consists of supplementary medical insurance (SMI), which *is not* financed by payroll taxes. SMI pays for physicians's services, outpatient hospital services, and other medical benefits, such as X-ray and radiation treatment, home dialysis equipment, diagnostic testing, but no prescriptions. This part of Medicare is voluntary, although persons eligible for HI are automatically enrolled when they attain 65. If they don't want the coverage, they must voluntarily refuse it. Medicare Part B is financed in part by monthly premiums paid by the beneficiaries and by the general revenues of the federal government. In 1996, premiums for SMI were $42.50 per month. In the same year, premiums paid for 22 percent of SMI benefits, general federal revenues 76 percent, and interest on securities held in the SMI trust fund the remaining 2 percent.[7] As with OASDI and HI, there is also a trust fund for SMI, into which all revenues under the program are paid, and from which all benefits are disbursed. At the end of 1996, assets of the SMI trust fund were $26.9 billion.[8]

Under Medicare, two methods are used to pay physicians. The first is called the *assignment* method. The physician accepts an assignment from the patient, and the payment is made directly by Medicare to the physician. Under this method the physician also agrees to accept the charge determined by Medicare as total payment for the service. The other method is called the *itemized bill* method. Under this method the patient or the physician files an itemized bill with Medicare, which in turn determines the approved charges and pays the patient directly 80 percent of those charges. If the physician's fee exceeds 80 percent of the approved charges, the patient must pay the balance.

Professor George Rejda of the University of Nebraska-Lincoln estimates that SMI covers only about 45 percent of the medical costs of the aged, a situation that has given rise to flourishing sales of "Medigap" insurance, policies designed to help bridge the gap between what Medicare pays and medical costs.[9] If a Medigap policy meets certain standards, it receives federal approval. Even the best of such policies, according to Professor Rejda, do not take full care of the Medicare gap because usually they don't cover prescription drugs or custodial care in nursing homes. Typically, a Medigap policy will pay around 20 percent of the approved charge.[10] Of course, if the physician accepts assignment for the claim, the patient avoids all extra charges.

The other major change that resulted from the 1965 amendments was the creation of an entirely new program of public assistance—Medicaid. This became Title XIX of the Social Security Act. Medicaid is a joint federal-state program to provide medical assistance to families with dependent children (AFDC), the aged, the blind, the disabled, and other persons in poverty. The law requires states to cover the *categorically needy,* which includes persons receiving cash benefits under AFDC and Supplementary Security Income (SSI), which in 1972 replaced existing programs of public assistance for the aged who are not receiving Social Security, for the blind, and for the disabled. Under Medicaid, states may also extend medical care to the *optional categorically needy,* which includes among others pregnant women and infants, and also to the *medically needy,* persons not covered by the cash assistance programs (AFDC and SSI), but whose incomes are sufficient to meet their basic living expenses, but insufficient to meet their medical expenses.[11]

All applicants for Medicaid must meet a needs test, which is basically the same as the means test established by the states for recipients of AFDC and SSI. Medicaid is financed jointly by the federal government and the states, using a formula that determines the federal share of a state's payments for medical services. Currently, the federal share varies between 50 and 83 percent of total costs, depending upon the state's per capita income. Poorer states receive a higher percentage of federal assistance for Medicaid spending than do the wealthier states.

The 1983 "Big Fix"

In 1975, for the first time since its beginning, Social Security (including disability income) ran a deficit, benefit payments exceeding income by $1,544 million. These deficits continued, reaching a staggering $12,198 million in 1982, when the Social Security Administration borrowed $12,437 million from the Medicare trust fund. Congress in 1981 had passed legislation that permitted borrowing among the various trust funds. Between 1975 and 1982, the combined OASI and DI trust funds were reduced by $21,347 million, a drastic 46.6 percent fall in their balances.[12] This series of deficits in the Social Security accounts caused alarm across the country. The press heard and repeated reports that Social Security was facing disaster in the twenty-first century as the baby boomers retired and the smaller baby-buster cohort would have to carry the burden of their retirement. Muttering about intergenerational warfare began to be heard.

In response to the growing concerns about the long-term viability of Social Security, the Reagan administration created by executive order in December, 1981, a bipartisan "blue ribbon" National Commission on Social Security Reform to analyze and to cope with the problem. The Commission consisted of fifteen members, five appointed by the president, five by the Republican congressional leadership, and five by the Democratic congressional leadership. It was headed by Alan Greenspan, current Chairman of the Federal Reserve, and a former member of President Ford's Council of Economic Advisers. Although Republicans dominated the Commission's membership, the final recommendations of the Commission were not excessively partisan.

Among the well-known members of the Commission in addition to Greenspan were Senators Robert Dole, Republican, and Daniel Patrick Moynihan, Democrat; Barber Conable, ranking Republican on the House Ways and Means Committee; Claude Pepper, former Democratic senator from Florida, and at the time a member of the House; Alexander Trowbridge, president of the National Association of Manufacturers; Robert M. Ball, former

Social Security Commissioner; and Lane Kirkland, then president of the AFL-CIO. The commission first met in February 1982, and continued regular meetings until mid-January 1983, when it reached agreement on a package of Social Security reforms that it transmitted to the administration, which in turn sent it to Congress without any significant changes.

Most important, perhaps, was the first and unanimous recommendation of the commission that the essential design of the Social Security system not be changed. Specifically, the commission said:

> The members of the National Commission believe that Congress . . . should not alter the fundamental structure of the Social Security program or undermine its fundamental principles. The national Commission considered, but rejected, proposals to make the Social Security program a voluntary one, or to transform it into a program under which benefits are a product exclusively of the contributions paid, or convert it into a fully funded program, or to change it to a program under which benefits are conditioned on the showing of financial need.[13]

Thus, Social Security would continue to be a pay-as-you-go transfer program in which the working population pays for the benefits and with its main features—universal contributions, universality of benefits, and no means testing—unchanged. With minor exceptions, Congress in early 1983 adopted the major recommendations of the commission. These included treating one-half of benefits as taxable income (now raised to 80 percent), expanding coverage to include newly hired federal employees and employees of nonprofit institutions, raising the retirement age to 67 by the year 2022, increasing the penalty for early retirement at age 62, delaying for six months a cost-of-living adjustment (COLA) for Social Security beneficiaries, increasing payroll taxes on the self-employed, and accelerating increases in the payroll tax already scheduled.

The 1983 "big fix" resulted in a quick and remarkable change in the financial situation for Social Security. In 1983, Social Security revenues jumped by 15.8 percent, while outlays for benefits increased by only 6.8 percent.[14] The 1983 changes, plus the small size of the depression-age cohort that began to retire in the 1990s, brought a drastic improvement in the Social Security financial picture. Between 1983 and 1989, the Social Security accounts had a surplus of $130,190 million, an amount which made it possible to repay fully the earlier loan of $12,437 million from the Medicare trust fund. By 1989, the trust fund balance had climbed back to $162,960 million, a 564 percent increase over the 1981 low of $24,539 million.[15] By 1998, the combined trust fund balance for OASI and DI was expected to reach $729,200 million.[16]

Here Come the Boomers

In Chapter 1 we sketched out the broad impact the coming retirement of the baby boomer cohort will have on the economy (measured by the GDP and the national income) and the taxes and spending of the federal government. Now it is appropriate in concluding this survey of the origin and development of the Social Security system to examine more closely the drastic demographic changes in store as the boomers enter retirement. Assuming 65 as the retirement age,[17] the first of the boomers will retire in 2010 and the last retire in 2030. As was noted in Chapter 1 (Table 1.5), the OASI and DI trust funds begin being rapidly depleted after 2015 and are exhausted by 2029, just before the last of the boomers enter retirement. As the boomers retire, far-reaching changes in the nation's population structure will result, changes that will have an enormous impact on almost every aspect of the nation's economic life. Because of the enormous size of the baby boomer cohort, the impact of the boomers on the nation's social insurance system will be unlike anything experienced to date. This is a demographic fact. The 76 million baby boomers are here, their retirement will take place, and the nation will have to cope with their impact on the Social Security system.

The bright side of this picture is the equally important fact of time. The crunch facing Social Security is real, but it is not immediate. Thus, the nation has the luxury of time to devise workable policies to make certain that Social Security—the "crown jewel" of American social insurance programs—remains viable for the retirement of the boomers in the next century.

One major change resulting from the boomers' retirement will be in the nation's population structure—a term demographers use to refer to the share of the total population found in different age brackets. Forecasting population change as far as seventy-five years or more into the future is not simply a matter of projecting recent trends into the years ahead. Population growth depends basically on three variables—the birth rate, mortality rates, and immigration, all of which are subject to variation, sometimes quite pronounced. Very small changes in birth and death rates can have very large effects upon future population.

Table 2.1 shows the distribution of actual and projected population totals by three major categories of people—under 20, 20 to 64, and 65 and over—for a 125-year period, from 1950 through 2075. The projections represent the best estimate by the Board of Trustees for the OASI and DI Trust Funds for changes in the nation's population structure between 1995 and 2075.

These data show clearly that a vast transformation in the population structure of the American economy is under way, one that will ultimately affect every single aspect of American life. It is a transformation from a society of youth to one of middle and older age—to what has been called "the graying of America." When the nation emerged from World War II, more than one-third of the population was under 20 years of age, while only 8 percent of Americans were 65 years of age or older. By 2075, if the Trustees' forecasts are correct, the over-65 and the under-20 population cohorts will be equal in their share of the total population.

The most dramatic shift is in the proportion of the population age 65 and older, a proportion that will nearly triple between 1950 and 2075. In 1950, there were only 12.8 million people over 65 living in the United States, but this number is forecast to explode to 85.9 million by 2075, a staggering 73.1 million increase! It would be difficult to imagine a more far-reaching trans-

Table 2.1

The Changing Population Structure for the United States: 1950–2075*
(in percent)

Year	Under 20	20–64	Over 65
	Historic data—1950–1995		
1950	33.8	58.2	8.0
1960	38.4	52.5	9.1
1970	37.6	52.7	9.7
	1960s and 1970s reflect the baby-boomer bulge		
1980	31.7	57.2	11.1
1990	28.9	58.8	12.3
1995	28.9	58.5	12.5
	Projected data—2000–2075		
2000	28.6	59.0	12.4
	Baby boomers enter retirement: 2010–2030		
2010	26.5	60.5	12.9
2020	24.9	58.9	16.2
2030	24.2	55.9	19.8
2040	23.5	55.9	20.6
2050	23.2	55.9	20.8
2060	23.0	55.2	21.9
2070	22.8	54.8	22.5
2075	22.7	54.6	22.7
Percent change	–32.8	–6.2	183.7
Annual rate of growth			
From 1950	0.40	0.65	1.55
From 1995	0.10	0.33	1.17

Source: 1997 Annual Report, Board of Trustees, Federal Old Age and Survivors Insurance and the Federal Disability Insurance Trust Funds.

*In proportion to the total population.

formation in the nation's population pattern, one that results from the inexorable movement through time of the 75 million-strong boomer cohort—from birth through childhood and primary school, into high school and college, young adulthood and family formation, entry into the workforce, and ultimately retirement.

Aside from the passage of the baby boomers through the various stages of the population structure, increased longevity is a major factor in the growth of the absolute and relative numbers of persons 65 years of age and older. Between 1940 and 1995, the life expectancy at birth for males went from 61.4 to 72.6 years, an 18.2 percent gain. For females, the change was from 65.7 years at birth to 79.0, a 20.2 percent increase. From 1995 through 2075, the added life expectancy for males at the age of 65 will rise from 15.6 to 18.8 and for females 19.0 to 22.3.[18] Male boomers who retire at age 65 between 2010 and 2030 can expect, on average, to live into their early 80s. The life-expectancy figures just cited are, of course, averages. Many boomers will live well beyond their statistical life span. In 1992, 10.1 percent of all persons over the age of 65 were 85 years or older. Some demographers believe this percentage will reach 13 percent by 2015, and possibly peak out at 24 percent in 2050.[19]

Until 2030, when the last of the boomers enter retirement, the projections show only a moderate increase in proportion of the population age 65 and older. After 2030, this ratio jumps up sharply, reaching a level of 22.7 percent of the population by 2075. Overall, the population share of persons 65 years and older grew and is forecast to grow by 183.7 percent. This does not translate into an extremely large annual rate of growth. For the entire period—1950 through 2075—the annual average rate of growth in the over 65 population is estimated at 1.55 percent. This rate, though, is greater than the actual and forecast total population growth rate for the period, which is 0.70 percent, or for the rates for the 20–64 age group, 0.65 percent, and the under 20 cohort of 0.40 percent.[20]

The low growth rate for the under-20 cohort reflects the drop in the fertility rate from a peak of 3.61 in 1960 to a low of 1.76 in 1978, a fall-off that gave rise to the baby-buster cohort.[21] The projected data show a continued drop in the fertility rate after 2000 for the nation's population to less than the replacement rate of 2.0. The situation gets a bit tricky here. Paradoxically, the total number of births has risen while the fertility rate has fallen. This is because the large increase in the number of boomer women in the childbearing age more than offset the drop-off in their fertility rate.

Another dimension of the population situation is the relationship between the labor force, OASI and DI recipients, and the population under 20. These relationships are shown in Table 2.2.

The numbers in this table that are the most worrisome and have been widely publicized are those showing the number of workers per beneficiary. This figure was abnormally high in 1945, because Social Security was in its infancy with relatively few beneficiaries. After 1950, however, the number of persons receiving benefits rapidly expanded. For the entire period, actual and projected OASI and DI beneficiaries grow at an annual average rate of 3.42 percent, a rate much in excess of the actual and forecast annual growth rate for the labor force (0.73 percent). From 2000 to 2075, the projected growth rate for beneficiaries remains far greater than the growth rate for the labor force—1.05 percent compared to 0.03 percent.

The result of these disparities in the growth of beneficiaries and of the labor force is a steady decline in the ratio of workers per retired and disabled persons and survivors. In 1960 there were 4.7 workers per OASI and DI beneficiary, but by 2075 there will be only 1.4 workers for each beneficiary. To put the matter differently, in 1960 for every 100 workers there were 21 persons receiving OASI and DI benefits, but by 1975 for every 100 workers there were 73 beneficiaries of OASI and DI.

In the minds of many critics the foregoing is the nub of the crisis facing Social Security in the next century—too few workers and too many beneficiaries for a viable system! Without drastic increases in taxes, severe cuts in benefits, or a combination of both, Social Security as it now exists cannot survive. At risk is what Alan Pifer calls "the traditional *unwritten* contract under which each generation supports the one above it in exchange for support in its old age by the generation below it."[22] This gets to the essence of our pay-as-you-go Social Security system. The gloomy numbers in Table 2.2 not only foretell a shattering of this unwritten contract, but also raise the warning flag of inter-

Table 2.2

OASI and DI Beneficiaries, Population Under 20, and the Civilian Labor Force for Selected Years: 1945–2075 (in millions and in percent)

Year	OASI and DI Recipi-ents	Under 20	Total Depen-dents*	Labor Force	Workers per Bene-ficiary	Depen-dents per 100 Workers
			Historic data			
1945	1.3	46.2	47.5	53.9	45.6	85
1950	3.5	53.9	57.4	62.2	17.8	92
1960	14.8	73.0	87.8	69.6	4.7	126
1970	25.7	80.7	106.4	82.8	3.2	129
1980	35.5	74.6	110.1	106.9	3.0	103
1990	39.8	75.1	114.9	125.8	3.2	91
1995	43.4	79.1	122.5	132.3	3.0	93
			Projected data			
2000	45.9	81.4	136.4	134.9	2.5	101
	Boomers enter retirement: 2010 through 2030					
2010	55.0	81.4	136.4	134.9	2.5	101
2020	69.6	81.8	151.4	135.2	1.9	112
2030	82.0	83.2	165.2	135.5	1.7	122
2040	86.2	87.3	169.5	135.8	1.6	124
2050	89.3	84.2	173.5	135.9	1.5	127
2060	94.3	84.9	179.2	136.0	1.4	131
2070	97.8	85.5	183.3	136.2	1.4	134
2075	99.6	85.8	185.4	136.3	1.4	135
Annual rates of change						
From 1945	3.42	0.48	1.08	0.73	—	—
From 1950	2.73	0.37	0.95	0.64	—	—
From 2000	1.05	0.07	0.51	0.03	—	—

Source: 1997 Annual Report, Board of Trustees of the Federal Old-Age and Survivors Insurance and the Federal Disability Insurance Trust Funds.

*Total dependents equals OASI and DI recipients plus persons under 20 years of age.

generational class warfare. The latter may happen if the baby busters and their children rebel against the taxes they will have to shoulder in order to give the boomers the same level of benefits that the parents of the boomers now enjoy. How to cope with this danger—which means, in effect, finding a way to "save Social Security"—is the challenge we shall tackle in Chapters 4 and 5.

Another dimension to the coming problem can be seen in the figures found in the last column of Table 2.2, which measures the number of dependents for each 100 workers. "Dependents" in this context includes OASI and DI beneficiaries plus all persons below the age of 20. The latter are an approximate proxy for children, even though some persons below 20 years in age are actually in the workforce. In 1945 there were 88 dependents for each 100 persons in the workforce. This number shot up significantly under the influence of the baby boomers, reaching a peak of 129 dependent persons in 1970 for each 100 workers. After that, reflecting the baby-bust generation, dependents per 100 workers dropped back to 93 by 1975. Then the projected data show this ratio rising again, quite sharply by 2020, the first year of retirement for the boomers, and continuing to rise up to 2075, when a peak of 135 dependents for each 100 persons in the labor force is reached. The reason for the continued rise in this ratio even after the last of the boomers has entered into retirement (2030) is the very low rates of growth projected for the labor force after 2030.

Why are such low rates of growth projected for the labor force? One reason is that the baby-bust generation and a falling fertility rate came together in the beginning of the 1970s to shrink the size of the working-age population in the 1980s and 1990s. Further, the OASI and DI Trustees expect the labor force participation rate for women to level off—nearly two-thirds of women are now in the labor force—and the rate for men to continue to decline. Since it was the increase in women in the labor force that kept the total labor force participation rate rising between 1950 and 1996, a leveling-off of the rate for women coupled with a continued decline in the rate for men will lower the overall rate. Table 2.3 shows the labor force participation rate for men, for women, and for both sexes at five year intervals since 1950.

Economists are unsure of the exact reasons for the decline in the labor force participation rate for men, although many believe the loss of blue-collar manufacturing jobs is a major reason why so many males dropped out of the labor force. Between 1950 and

Table 2.3

Labor Force Participation Rates* for Men, Women, and Both Sexes: 1950–1996 (in percent)

Period	Men	Women	Both Sexes
1950–1954	86.1	34.4	59.0
1955–1959	84.7	36.7	58.9
1960–1964	82.1	38.1	59.9
1965–1969	80.3	41.0	59.7
1970–1974	79.0	44.2	60.6
1975–1979	77.8	48.6	62.4
1980–1984	76.8	52.5	64.0
1985–1989	76.3	55.9	65.6
1990–1994	75.7	57.9	66.4
1995–1996	74.9	59.1	66.7
Percent change	–13.0	71.8	13.1

Source: Economic Report of the President, 1997.

*Labor force participation rates is the civilian labor force as a percent of the noninstitutional civilian population.

1996, employment in manufacturing grew by only 19.9 percent, far less than the 164.5 percent increase in total employment, the 267.0 percent gain in services employment, and the 244.4 percent rise in government employment, the overwhelming proportion of which was at the state and local level. The latter grew by 307.6 percent between 1950 and 1996, whereas federal employment grew by only 43.0 percent.[23]

The Boomers and the Culture of Aging

Forecasting the economic and demographic changes that the baby boomers will bring about as they enter their retirement years is relatively straightforward as compared to forecasting their impact on the cultural aspects of the aging process in America. What is certain is that the boomers in retirement will affect the aging stage of the life cycle just as profoundly as they have affected all of America's social, economic, and political institutions on their way through the earlier stages of their lives.

Now entering into their 50s, the boomers are approaching retirement as, perhaps, the best educated, the healthiest, and most affluent generation in American history. Known, too, as the "me generation," the boomers will not be shy about letting their needs and wants be known, including an adequate income in their retirement years. There is little doubt that their numbers will give them enormous political clout, but unless they begin now to use their power wisely, the resources may not be there to give them in retirement the lifestyle to which they believe they are entitled.

It is quite possible that out of this will come a changed attitude toward government, a switch away from the indifferent or even hostile attitude now held by a majority of the boomers, especially the highly visible "Yuppies." As the boomers approach the retirement years, many will begin to see how important Social Security will be for their own retirement. One reason why this may happen is because a growing chorus of voices is warning the boomers of the dire consequences awaiting them because they are not saving adequately for their own retirement. This is likely to turn them into strong supporters of Social Security, especially Medicare, an experience that Kevin Phillips, author of *The Politics of Rich and Poor* (New York: Random House, 1990) thinks may lead many boomers to adopt more of a pro-government stance. As the boomers age, issues of aging will increasingly dominate the political landscape, issues which, the boomers will learn, must be resolved at the governmental level.

One of the most powerful forces shaping our society is advertising, especially television advertising. It is a force that helps define who we are and what we want to be. Even though government has a critical and enlarged role in the contemporary American economy, America remains overwhelmingly a consumer-led, market-based economy. For much of the post–World War II era, youthful beauty, youthful vigor, youthful tastes, and youthful health has been the dominant theme in the torrent of advertising flowing out of Madison Avenue into American homes through television, radio, slick paper magazines, and newspapers. A few years ago the middle-aged, not to mention the old, were rarely seen in the ads, but this is changing. Madison Avenue and the corporate giants that produce and sell the billions of dollars worth of goods and services that Americans consume are aware that the largest bloc of consumers in the American economy—the 75 million baby-boomers—are entering their 50s. Increasingly, mass advertising will reflect and adjust to this fact. Further, as Madison Avenue did when the boomers dominated the youth culture, advertising in the ways it portrays middle age will help shape the boomers perception of themselves in this stage of their life cycle.

The relationship between work, leisure, and retirement is another area where traditional notions and practices will change, quite possibly in totally unexpected ways. Many boomers, as they enter their 60s and get closer to actual retirement, may want to work longer, given their good health and the paucity of their savings from earlier years. Yet, these desires may collide with recent corporate practices such as downsizing, which is mostly directed at older workers. If it turns out that significant numbers of boomers want to work beyond the traditional retirement age—some in their 50s may even want to start second careers—but there are not enough jobs, they will have to look to the government for help. From the standpoint of the stresses the Social Security system is facing as the boomers enter retirement, working longer on the part of many of the boomers would be a healthy development, providing the jobs can be found. Boomers born in 1960 and later will have to wait until they are 67 to get their full retirement benefits, since the normal retirement age will be raised to 67 by 2027. Some observers believe that the matter is not so serious because the "baby-bust" generation following the boomers will lead to a scarcity of workers, inducing business firms to hold on to their older workers. In any event, the nature of work is changing, with the distinction between work and retirement becoming blurred.

The good health of the boomers is yet another factor that will change our notions of what retirement is—or should be. Many boomers will be able to remain physically active well into their 70s—and even their 80s in some cases. With added years of leisure because of a greater longevity, travel, and continuing education will be a major part of life for many of the boomers. The Elder Hostel movement, which combines education and travel, has blossomed for the parents of the baby boomers, and as the boomers reach retirement it may almost literally explode in the magnitude and scope of its activities. One of the major growth industries of the late twentieth century involves the pleasure cruise. The transatlantic liners may be practically extinct, but the cruise ship industry is enjoying enormous growth, a trend that will undoubtedly accelerate as the boomers retire.

Alvin Toffler, author of *Future Shock* (1970) and *The Third Wave* (1980), sees the boomers not as a monolithic mass, but as a generation still influenced by the experience of the 1960s, when "do your own thing" was the upbeat slogan of the day. Thus, the boomers will bring diversity and individuality to retirement, refusing to conform to any stereotypes, and not easily captured politically by either of the nation's two major parties.[24]

The changes, if they come about, will mean a richer and more challenging culture, not just for the boomers in their retirement, but for the entire society. But there is no certainty that this is the direction society will move as the boomers enter into retirement. The reality is that the boomers are facing two widely different futures, one of prosperity, intergenerational peace and goodwill, and ample opportunity for young and old alike to pursue their version of the American dream. Alternatively, there may be stagnation, open and bitter hostility between the generations, a society racked by intolerance and hatred.

Ironically, which of the forgoing futures will prevail depends upon the boomers themselves! As we approach the end of this century, the boomers are in the most productive phase of their lives, their 40s and early 50s. Thus the future, including the survival and viability of Social Security, is going to be shaped by decisions made now and in the early years of the twenty-first century. There is no other way. The ball truly is in the court of the "me generation."

— 3 —

Things Are Not What They Seem: How Social Security Works

Our nation's Social Security system has been in existence for sixty-three years, yet many Americans—possibly a majority—don't really understand how the system works, or how they personally fit into the system, both as taxpayers and as persons who one day will receive benefits from it. In this chapter we take an in-depth look at the workings of the system. First, though, some comments are in order about a major misconception, namely that Social Security is wholly analogous to a private pension or annuity plan. After that comes an explanation of the mechanics of the system, followed by analyses of other widely-held misunderstandings and criticisms.

Social Security and Private Pensions

Perhaps the most serious error is equating Social Security with a private pension or annuity. They are not the same. In a private pension scheme found in many business firms, the employee contributes a specific percentage of his or her salary to a fund, usually administered by the organization for which the employee works. Sometimes, but not always, the individual's employer will match the employee's contribution. In any event, the amounts coming from the employee and the employer are normally invested by the pension managers in the name of the employee in financial instruments. These may be private bonds, stocks (equities), and government securities, including interest-yielding obligations of state and local governments, as well as those of the federal government. Most pension funds are diversified and contain varying amounts of each of the foregoing securities.

The key element in this picture is the fund. Its magnitude and value, which depends on the contributions by the employee and employer plus the interest and dividend income earned by the securities in the fund, determines the size of the pension that an employee will receive when he or she enters retirement. Employees may or may not have a say in the kind of financial assets in which the managers of the fund invest. Further, the fund that an employee accumulates with a particular firm may or may not be "portable," which means that the fund follows the employee when he or she takes a job with a different employer. In the final analysis, what counts for any private pension is the size and value of a fund accumulated in the name of the employee over a person's lifetime employment.

Social Security is fundamentally different, although a large number of persons persist in believing that Social Security works in the same manner as private pension schemes. In part, this is because the language used to describe Social Security is similar to the language used in conjunction with private pensions. Terms like "insurance," "accounts," "trust funds," and "contributions" are often used by the government to describe Social Security, but this leads to confusion because these terms are also applicable to private pensions. As a matter of fact, such words are more appropriately applied to private pensions than to Social Security.

Another source of confusion is the practice of some scholars and critics of calculating a hypothetical "rate of return" on the taxes a worker has paid into Social Security over his working life. Technically, this involves a comparison between the present value of a worker's expected benefits and the present value of expected contributions. The implication of this is that the worker really is paying into a fund, of which the size and the rate of interest will determine his benefits. But this is not the case. Since workers may enter Social Security at different stages in their working lives, the procedure is flawed. For example, an older worker who joined the system late in his or her career, but received full benefits, would receive a very high rate of return, whereas younger workers who paid into the system throughout their entire working life get a much lower return. This practice overlooks the fact that Social Security is far more than an investment program. It is a system of social insurance that provides not only for retirement, but protection for workers and their families when the wage earner suffers a disability or a premature death.

The truly fundamental way in which Social Security differs from private pensions is in being an income transfer system, organized and administered by the federal government. What the government does is tax one segment of the population and quite literally *transfer* the money collected to another segment of the population. This is the bedrock essence of Social Security. The segment of the population being taxed is persons at work, and the segment of the population receiving this money includes persons over 65, disabled, and survivors of workers. Basically, Social Security is an *intergenerational* program, through which the federal government transfers income from the working population to the retired population, including the disabled and survivors. This means, again in a fundamental sense, that it is a "pay-as-you-go" (PAYG) system. Further, and unlike private pension systems, the transfer income (i.e., benefits) paid to the system's beneficiaries *are not* determined by what a worker has paid into the system in taxes over his or her working life, but by a government formula—called the "benefit formula"— which is based on the worker's lifetime earnings.

Throughout most of Social Security's sixty-three years of existence, taxes paid into the system were roughly equal to benefits paid out, with a small cushion held in reserve in the System's trust funds. As noted in Chapter 2, this situation underwent a drastic change in 1983 following the "Big Fix," which accelerated scheduled increases in the payroll taxes that finance Social Security. As a result of these changes, the balance in the combined OASI and DI trust funds was expected to reach a staggering $1.5 trillion by 2015.[1] The rapid growth in the surpluses in the Social Security accounts has not only focused attention on gigantic sums being accumulated in the trust funds, but also given rise to the drive to "privatize" a part of Social Security by investing some of these sums in the stock market. By law any surplus in the Social Security accounts must be invested in a special kind of Treasury (i.e., federal) security.

The persistence of public misunderstanding about the true nature of the Social Security system has several consequences, the most important of which are discussed in detail in Chapter 5 on "How to Save Social Security." But one particular consequence needs comment at this point. This is the belief that the surpluses in the Social Security Trust Funds (OASI and DI funds) are being "raided" to finance other government programs. This belief is widespread and is the rationale for a number of organizations that have sprung into existence and field vigorous campaigns to get legislation passed by Congress which will presumably end the raids on the trust funds.

Typical of these organizations is the United Seniors Association, Inc. (USA, Inc.) of Fairfax, VA, which in dramatic and alarming letters aimed at seniors and near-seniors pleads for funds "to stop the raid of the Social Security Trust Fund."[2] Claiming 640,000 members, USA, Inc. attempts to rally 1 million seniors to flood the Congress with letters and cards in support of this goal. Toward this end, Senator Sam Brownback of Kansas introduced in the Senate a bill entitled The Social Security Preservation Act, for which USA, Inc., is beating the drums. Presumably, this bill will stop Congress and the Social Security administration from spending any Social Security surplus on other government programs as is now done by using the surplus to purchase special, nonmarketable Treasury securities. When the Social Security Administration purchases these securities, funds flow into the Treasury that can be used for any government program. What this proposed legislation would do is require the Social Security Administration to invest any or all surpluses in either marketable Treasury bills, and/or FDIC-insured Certificates of Deposit. Then, according to USA, Inc., the trust funds "would contain *real assets,* not IOUs from the government itself."[3]

The choices selected by USA, Inc., for the investment of Social Security surpluses are curious. If some of the surplus is invested in Treasury bills, the funds will flow into the Treasury and become part of overall government spending just as they now do when invested in special nonmarketable Treasury securities. It is difficult to see any advantage in this arrangement, especially since interest rates are lower on Treasury bills than on the Treasury securities in which the surplus is now being invested. There would be some saving on interest costs to the government—the interest on the invested Social Security surplus is an *intragovernmental* transfer—but once benefit payments begin to exceed Social Security tax income plus interest, this saving would disappear and the government would have to make up the shortfall. Further, since Treasury bills are marketable, their value fluctuates, which introduces an element of instability and potential for loss into the situation.

As for investment in FDIC-insured Certificates of Deposit this really means that any surplus in the Social Security accounts is being deposited in the commercial banking system, where it may become the basis for an expansion of commercial bank lending and the money supply. This would probably have a greater inflationary impact on the economy than would the spending of the surplus more directly by the federal government. It is hard to see that this has any great economic advantage over current arrangements.

Peter G. Peterson, Founding President of the Concord Coalition, and Secretary of Commerce under President Nixon, has leveled extremely harsh criticism against the trust funds and their investment in special Treasury obligations. These "investments," he says, are nothing more than Treasury IOUs, or claims on future taxpayers, which the Treasury will have to redeem when they come due, by either borrowing, taxing the public, or both.

Worse yet, the awful truth, according to Peterson, is that Social Security "is a vast Ponzi scheme in which only the first people in are the big winners and the vast array of those who join late in the game lose."[4]

What leads Peterson to this harsh judgment is the fact that Social Security is an ongoing system that guarantees benefits to the future aged population without accumulating funds out of which these benefits can be paid, as is done with private pension schemes. These future benefits are the "unfunded liabilities" of the system, liabilities that will have to be met by future taxpayers. This, of course, is true, but this result is inherent in the basic pay-as-you-go nature of Social Security. The existence or nonexistence of an accumulated fund is not what counts with respect to the future viability of Social Security. What counts is the future health of the economy. Because Social Security is basically an income transfer system, its ultimate viability depends upon the growth in the economy and its productivity in the next century. This is a matter we shall explore in depth in Chapter 5, "How to Save Social Security." Now, by examining the way in which Social Security as a system actually works, we not only lay the groundwork for this discussion, but can judge whether, in fact, as Peter G. Peterson says, Social Security really is a Ponzi scheme.

How Social Security Works

A picture, the Chinese say, is worth 1,000 words. A flowchart type of diagram may or may not qualify as a picture, but such a diagram is very useful for explaining in a capsule way the workings of the Social Security system. Such a diagram is found in Figure 3.1, which uses 1996 data to trace the flow of money through the system, a simple and direct way not only to provide a quick and accurate explanation of how the system actually works, but also to reveal the essential nature of the system. The totals shown are for combined OASDI and DI operations. The rest of the Social Security program, namely Medicare, parts A and B, is not included. Only Part A of Medicare (HI) is financed

Figure 3.1 **How Social Security Works: Combined OASI and DI Funds** (billions of dollars in 1996)

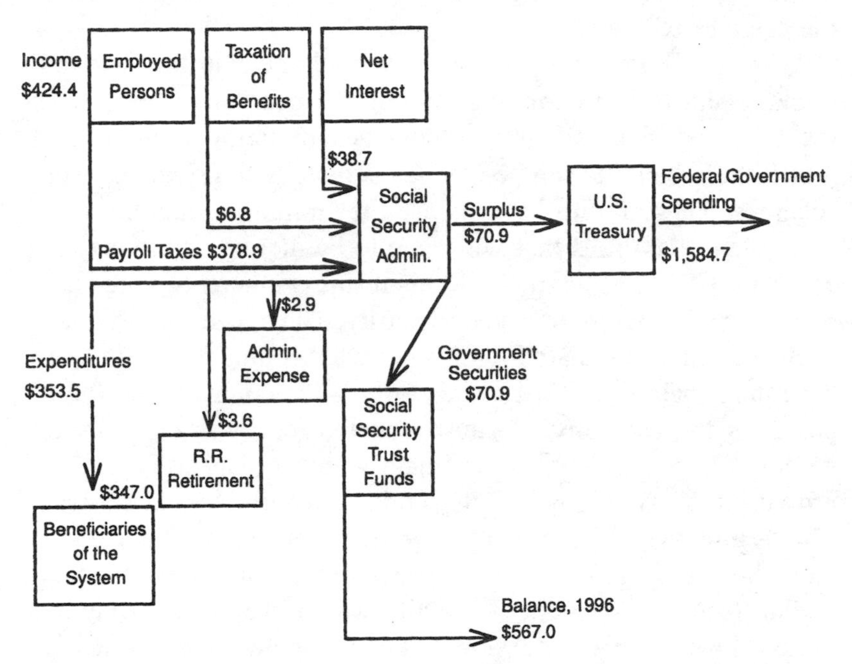

Source: Board of Trustees, Federal Old Age and Survivors Insurance and Disability Trust Funds.

by payroll taxes. Part B, SMI, which covers physician's services, outpatient services, and other medical services for the aged and disabled—is financed partly by premiums paid by covered persons, general revenues, and interest on balances in the SMI trust fund. As noted earlier, any surplus from Social Security operations *must* be invested in a special government security, technically called a *special public debt obligation.* These securities, which pay interest, are redeemable at any time at par by the Social Security Administration. The rate of interest they pay is equal to the average rate on all United States outstanding marketable securities not due to mature for at least four years from the date at which the rate is being determined.[5] Thus, the rate depends on average rate in a mix of ten- and thirty-year federal government bonds. In 1996, the effective annual rate of interest earned by assets in the trust funds was 7.7 percent. The interest income becomes a part of the Social Security Administration's overall income, which is used to pay benefits in each year.

In 1996 there were 122 million persons employed in "covered" occupations, that is, working at jobs which require both employees and employers to pay the social security tax. Because many persons held two or more jobs, the number of persons paying Social Security taxes was 144 million. In 1996, covered employment was 96 percent of total employment, including the self-employed. The fact that Social Security taxes were paid by 144 million people when actual employment was 122 million out of a civilian labor force of 136 million means that many people worked at more than one job, which suggests that a single job was not adequate for a desired standard of living, even when more than one person in a family worked.

In 1996 OASI and DI trust funds collected $378.9 billion from payroll taxes and $6.8 billion from taxation of benefits. Interest earned on the trust fund securities was $38.7 billion, leading to a total income of $424.4 billion. Benefits paid plus administrative expenses for the Social Security Administration totaled $353.6 billion. Income exceeded the benefits paid by $70.8 billion. The assets held in the OASI and DI trust fund are increased by the amount of this surplus. Consequently, at the close of 1996, the combined OASI and DI trust funds had assets of $567.0 billion.[6] The actual money itself (i.e., the dollar total of the surplus) goes to the Treasury, where it becomes a part of the general stream of income flowing into the Treasury in any one year, and is available for spending as jointly determined by Congress and the administration in power. If, by waving a magic wand, we could actually trace the path of specific Social Security tax dollars paid by a worker and his or her employer, we would find that ultimately these dollars may help pay for a tank for the army, an airplane for the air force, the salary of a supreme court justice, the paving of a highway in Iowa, a welfare check for a mother, or any other of the many hundreds of activities carried on by the U.S. government.

It is the foregoing scenario that is the basis for the anguished cries of the United Seniors Association, Inc., and like groups that "they are spending our money," and "It's time to put an end to Congress' 'raids' on the Social Security Trust funds."[7] In the same vein, these groups demand that the surpluses currently being generated by the system be set aside to be used only to pay Social Security benefits, instead of being invested, as the USA, Inc., says, in ". . . phony government IOUs." Further, the USA, Inc., asserts, if the surpluses are invested in negotiable Treasury bills and Certificates of Deposit from FDIC insured banks, the OASI and DI trust funds will hold "real" assets.[8]

These points require careful consideration, especially because they have much currency with senior and near-senior citizens. Consider this matter of "setting aside" the surpluses so they can be used to pay future benefits. What does this mean? How can it be done in a practical sense? The government might quite literally take the cash and checks it gets from the payroll taxes, turn the checks into cash, and put it all away in a vault, guarded heavily like we guard the gold at Fort Knox. But this would be absurd. The cash stashed away in a vault wouldn't bring the government any interest income, and, further as time passed and prices increased, its *real* (i.e., purchasing power) value would fall, hardly a desirable outcome.

So that leaves investment of the money as the only alternative. But, investment in what? As noted earlier, by law the Social Security Administration must invest any surplus in special public debt obligations, debts that USA, Inc. describes as "phony government IOUs." But consider this: of all the securities, public and private, that anyone may invest money in, what kinds of securities are considered the safest? Corporate bonds? Corporate stocks? Money market funds? Home mortgages? State and local government securities? Or obligations of the federal government? Federal government obligations head the list, the reason being that they are backed by the full faith and credit of the government of the United States. No other security has such a secure backing.

It is far from clear why critics of the trust funds regard investment in Treasury bills or certificates of deposit from commercial bank as more "real" than the special Treasury securities in which the fund now invests. Actually, in one sense the special Treasury securities may be more "real" than the marketable alternatives proposed by USA and other organizations. This is because the Social Security Administration can redeem these securities at their par value *at any time.* So there isn't any risk of a capital loss if the securities are redeemed before their normal maturity, as is not the case with securities that are marketable. Since the stability and safety of Social Security funds is a primary objective, avoiding unforeseen capital losses (or capital gains) is a desirable state of affairs.

One other point of criticism is worth mentioning. This is the demand that the Social Security trust funds be taken "off budget," which is to say that in governmental accounting they not be included in the unified federal budget that shows the total for *all* taxes and spending by the federal government. Because the federal government has been running a deficit every year since 1969, it is argued that throwing the trust funds with their surpluses in with other government spending and taxing totals masks the true size of the federal deficit. This is true, although the President's Council of Economic Advisers and the Joint Economic Committee of Congress calculate federal receipts and expenditures both with and without the Social Security and other trust funds. For example, in fiscal year 1997, the overall deficit was –$21.9 billion, but if the trust funds are excluded, the deficit becomes –$103.3 billion.[9] From the perspective of economic policy, what counts is the total flow of spending and taxes by the federal government. Consequently, for policy purposes the budget that shows the total income and outgo—including the trust funds—is best.

Operation of the Trust Funds

Dating back to the first years of Social Security, the trust funds are an integral part of the system. Primarily, they trace the flow of money into and out of the Social Security system. But they do more than this. The Social Security Act established a Board of Trustees to oversee the operations of the social insurance programs and the trust funds, of which there are now four. There is the OASI Trust Fund, the DI Trust Fund, the HI or Medicare, Part A Trust Fund, and SMI or Medicare Part B Trust Fund. Four of the six members of the Board of Trustees are on the Board by virtue of their position in the Federal government. They are: the Secretary of the Treasury (managing trustee); the Secretary of Labor; the Secretary of Health and Human Services; and the Commissioner of Social Security. The other two members are appointed by the president and confirmed by the Senate to serve as Public Trustees. The Social Security Act requires that the Trustees report annually to Congress on the financial and actuarial status of the trust funds.

The Trustees' annual reports to Congress on the financial condition of the trust funds contain projections of the future income, the outgo, and balances in the trust funds. Three alternative sets of projections are made, described as "low-cost," "intermediate," and "high-cost." They are intended to illustrate a reasonable range of outcomes. The "intermediate" set of projections represents the Trustees' best estimate of expected future economic and demographic trends, and is the set used in this book. The report to Congress examines both a short-range and a long-range outlook over a seventy-five-year valuation period. Reports for the OASI and DI Trust Funds make projections through 2075, and for the HI and SMI Trust Funds through 2070.[10]

Values for seven economic and six demographic variables are estimated for each of the three alternative projections—low-cost, intermediate, and high-cost. The economic variables include annual average percentage changes in: (1) real gross domestic product (GDP), (2) the average annual wage in covered employment,

Table 3.1

Actual and Estimated Values for Key Economic Variables for Selected Years: 1960–2075 (in percent)

	Average annual percentage change in:					Annual:	
	1 Real GDP	2 Annual average wage in current employment	3 Consumer Price Index	4 Real wage differential	5 Labor force	6 Interest rate	7 Unemployment rate
1960–64	4.6	3.4	1.2	2.2	1.3	3.7	5.7
1965–69	4.2	6.1	3.9	2.2	2.1	5.2	3.8
1975	–0.6	6.7	9.1	–2.4	1.9	7.4	8.5
1980	–0.3	9.4	13.4	–4.0	1.9	11.0	7.1
1985	3.7	4.7	3.5	1.2	1.7	10.8	7.2
1990	1.3	5.1	5.2	–0.1	0.7	8.6	5.5
1995	2.0	3.9	2.9	1.0	0.9	6.9	5.6
2000	2.0	4.3	3.4	0.9	1.0	6.7	5.8
2005	2.0	4.5	3.5	1.0	0.9	6.4	6.0
2010	1.8	4.5	3.5	1.0	0.7	6.2	6.0
2020	1.3	4.4	3.5	0.9	0.2	6.2	6.0
2030	1.4	4.4	3.5	0.9	0.2	6.2	6.0
2040	1.4	4.4	3.5	0.9	0.2	6.2	6.0
2050	1.3	4.4	3.5	0.9	0.1	6.2	6.0
2070	1.3	4.4	3.5	0.9	0.1	6.2	6.0
2075	1.3	4.4	3.5	0.9	0.1	6.2	6.0

Source: 1997 Annual Report, Board of Trustees of the Federal Old-Age and Survivors Insurance and the Federal Disability Trust Funds (Washington, DC: U.S. Government Printing Office, 1997).

(1) The real wage differential is the difference between the percentage increase in the annual average wage in employment (columns), and the percentage increase in the consumer price index (column 3). A positive value means an increase in the real wage.

(3) the consumer price index, (4) the real wage differential, which is the difference between percentage changes in the average annual wage in covered employment, and the consumer price index (CPI), and (5) the labor force. Annual average values are estimated for: (6) the interest rate, and (7) the unemployment rate. Table 3.1 shows actual and estimated values for selected years for these variables from 1960 through 2075.

As we shall note critically in Chapters 4 and 5, the projected values for these variables are crucial not only to estimates of future income, output, and trust fund balances, but also for defining precisely the problems that face Social Security in the twenty-first century. Particularly important are the low rates of growth projected for the real GDP after the year 2000. These rates, which are significantly below both recent and long-term averages for GDP growth, are an aspect of the Trustee's forecasts that we shall examine carefully in Chapter 4. Since GDP growth is a key determinant of how much income and output a society can transfer to its nonworking population, these low growth figures are also a major reason why trouble is projected for the Social Security system in the next century. Further, after 2005 little or no change is shown for most of the estimated data, a fact that simply reflects the difficulty of making projections far into the future.

The demographic variables include the total fertility rate, an age- and sex-adjusted death rate, and for males and females life expectancy at birth, and life expectancy at age 65. The demographic projections are crucial for estimating the size and composition of the future population that will be receiving benefits but also the population from which the labor force will be drawn. Table 3.2 shows for selected years actual and estimated values for the demographic values from 1960 through 2075.

The figures in Table 3.2—both actual and projected—inform us of a number of important and interesting population developments, both in the recent past and in the projected future. These developments are key factors in shaping Social Security's future. For example, they show significant decreases in both the fertility rate for women and the death rate for all persons. Between 1960 and 1995, the fertility rate declined by 44 percent, and it is expected to decline by another 6 percent between 1995 and 2075. The death rate for all persons fell by 67.6 percent between 1960 and 1995, and it is expected to fall by another 63.2 percent by 2075. These two trends translate into growing numbers of persons in upper ages in comparison to smaller numbers in the younger age brackets.

Table 3.2

Actual and Estimated Values for Key Demographic Variables for Selected Years: 1960–2075 (persons and years)

Year	Fertility rate[1]	Death rate[2]	Life Expectancy in Years: At birth, Male	At birth, Female	At age 65, Male	At age 65, Female
1960	3.61	1,237	66.7	73.2	12.9	15.9
1965	2.88	1,211	66.8	73.8	12.9	16.3
1970	2.43	1,138	67.1	74.9	13.1	17.1
1975	1.77	1,021	68.7	76.6	13.7	18.0
1980	1.05	961	69.9	77.5	14.0	18.4
1985	1.84	912	71.1	78.2	14.4	18.6
1990	2.07	866	71.8	78.9	15.0	19.0
1995	2.02	850	72.4	79.0	15.3	19.0
1997	2.03	823	72.9	79.3	15.6	19.2
2000	2.00	805	73.2	79.7	15.8	19.3
2005	1.97	772	74.1	80.1	16.0	19.5
2010	1.95	747	74.7	80.5	16.2	19.6
2020	1.90	704	75.5	81.1	16.6	20.0
2030	1.90	665	76.8	82.4	17.5	20.9
2040	1.90	598	77.5	82.9	17.8	21.3
2050	1.90	598	77.5	82.9	17.8	21.3
2070	1.90	542	78.6	84.0	18.6	22.1
2075	1.90	530	78.9	84.3	18.8	22.3

Sources: 1998 Annual Report, Board of Trustees of the Federal Old-Age and Survivors Insurance and the Federal Disability Insurance Trust Funds, (Washington, DC: U.S. Government Printing Office, 1998).

[1]Average number of children born to a woman in her lifetime during the childbearing period.

[2]Deaths per 100,000 persons.

These projections are reinforced by the figures on life expectancy. Table 3.2 shows significant increases in life expectancy for both males and females at birth and at age 65, with gains for males being slightly larger than gains for females. Between 1960 and 1997, the life expectancy for males at birth rose by 9.3 percent, while that of females increased by 8.3 percent. For the years after 1997 and through 2075, the at-birth life expectancy of males is expected to increase by 8.2 percent, and for females, 6.3 percent. There have been even greater changes in life expectancy at age 65 for both males and females, a development reflecting important and expected advances in medical care for the aged. Between 1960 and 1997, the life expectancy for men aged 65 jumped by 20.9 percent, and it is expected to rise by another 20.5 percent between 1995 and 2075. For women, the comparable percentages are 20.8 and 16.1. Clearly these figures foresee an aging America, one in which a rising proportion of the population will depend in whole or in part on Social Security as its source of income.

Economic Condition of the Trust Funds

Several different kinds of calculations and projections are made to show the economic condition of the trust funds over the periods contained in each report. One important number is the "trust fund ratio," which is the ratio of the fund at the beginning of the year to expected expenditures during the year. This ratio is the primary measure of a fund's financial adequacy in the short range. For example, the 1997 Trustees' Report shows that the combined OASI and DI ratio will reach a high of 265 percent by 2011, and then fall to zero by 2029. When the latter happens, the combined OASI and DI funds will be exhausted.[11] Since the Trustees view the short range as the next ten years, these projections show that the funds meet the short-range test for financial adequacy through 2025, when the ratio becomes 100 percent, meaning assets are just equal to expenditures. After that, fund assets continually fall short of expenditures until they are exhausted in 2029.

For the long-range status of the trust funds, two concepts are important, the "income rate" and the "cost rate," both calculated on an annual basis. The annual income rate is the ratio of trust fund income to taxable payroll for each year, and the cost rate is the ratio of trust fund outgo or expenditure to taxable payroll each year. These ratios are, of course, percentages—income and outgo as percents of taxable income. The difference between the

Table 3.3

Income and Cost Rates for the Combined OASI and DI Trust Funds for Selected Years: 1997–2075 (in percent)

Year	Combined OASI and DI Trust Funds		
	Income rate	Cost rate	Balance
1997	12.63	11.49	1.14
2000	12.64	11.73	0.91
2005	12.67	11.98	0.70
2010	12.73	12.48	0.26
2020	12.92	15.14	–2.22
2030	13.09	17.47	–4.38
2040	13.16	17.78	–4.61
2050	13.21	17.97	–4.76
2060	13.28	18.72	–5.45
2070	13.32	19.18	–5.86
2075	13.34	19.42	–6.07

Source: 1997 Annual Report, Board of Trustees of the Federal Old-Age and Survivors Insurance and the Federal Disability Trust Funds (Washington, DC: U.S. Government Printing Office, 1997).

income and cost rates is called the annual balance. Table 3.3 shows for selected years between 1997 and 2075 for the combined OASI and DI trust fund projections of the income rate, the cost rate, and the annual balance.

These projections show that income rates increase slowly and steadily because of the combination of the flat payroll tax—projections are based upon the tax rates in effect in 1998—and the increasing effect of the taxation of benefits. Costs as a percentage of taxable payrolls are expected to rise slowly through 2020, and then to increase rapidly until 2030, when the last of the baby boomers enter retirement. After that they slow down as the baby boomers age and die and the smaller baby-bust generation enters retirement.

In the projections contained in Table 3.3, the income rate does not include interest on the assets held in the trust funds. What the income rate reflects is income derived solely from taxation—the payroll tax and taxes on benefits. Excluding interest on trust fund assets—money that must come from the Treasury, and thereby from within the government—gives us a precise percentage figure by which tax-generated income falls short of the benefits paid out each year. This information is useful for looking at the shortfall in OASI and DI income in any one year, but it doesn't tell us how much current taxes should be increased to bring the income and cost ratios into balance.

To elaborate, Table 3.3 shows that the forecast tax (i.e., income) rate falls short of the cost rate by 6.07 percent in 2075, but this does not mean the payroll tax should immediately be increased by that many percentage points. Table 3.3 simply shows with the *present payroll tax* whether the tax rate exceeds or falls short of the cost rate in each year. After 2020, as Table 3.3 shows, taxes fall short of outgo, so this is the year in which the trust fund balances begin to decline. What we need to know is how much of an increase in the payroll tax *is currently needed* to keep the fund in balance up to 2075? To answer this question the Trustees calculate what they call the "actuarial balance" of the funds. The actuarial balance for a specified period—say, 1997–2075—is defined as the difference between the *summarized income rate* and the *summarized cost rate.* These rates are defined as follows:

> *The Summarized Income Rate* is: the ratio of (a) the sum of the trust fund value at the beginning of the period plus the present value of the total income (excluding interest income) during the period to (b) the present value of taxable payrolls during the period.
>
> *The Summarized Cost Rate* is: the ratio of (a) the sum of the present value of outgo during the period plus the present value of a targeted fund level at the end of the period equal to the following year's outgo to (b) the present value of taxable payrolls during the period.

Matters can get a bit confusing at this point. But keep in mind that the straight income and cost rates pertain to taxes and expenditures as a percent of taxable income *for a single year.* The summarized income and cost rates represent tax income and expenditures as percentages of taxable income *over a specified period,* such as 1997–2021, or 1997–2075. They also incorporate calculations of the present value of the trust fund balances at the beginning of a period and the required size of the trust fund at the end of the period. The latter must be large enough to meet the following year's expenditures for Social Security benefits.

In calculating present value in the foregoing exercise, the Trustees use the rate of interest assumed for calculating the interest earnings of the trust funds over the projected period. This is how interest income is brought into the picture. A level of assets in the trust funds equal to one year's expenditure is considered by the Social Security Administration as an adequate reserve for unforeseen contingencies. This is the targeted level of the trust funds for the ending of any period.

The Social Security program is in actuarial balance when the difference between the summarized income and cost rate is zero. If the actuarial balance is negative, it means that estimated future income plus the beginning trust fund balance are not sufficient to cover estimated expenditure and end up with a level of assets sufficient to cover one year's expenditure. This is a signal that the program can expect financial problems in the future and that action should be taken to correct the situation. If, however, the actuarial balance is positive, then the income will be sufficient to cover all projected expenditure and end up with assets greater than the targeted level of one year's outlay.

Table 3.4 compares estimates of summarized income and cost rates and the actuarial balance of the combined OASI and DI trust funds for five income period of differing lengths.

These numbers show that for the near term (1997–2011), there is a positive actuarial balance in the funds, but soon after this date, the balance becomes not only negative, but increasingly out of balance. For the entire seventy-five-year period from 1997 to 2071, the actuarial balance is –2.23. What does this number mean? Essentially, it is the percentage amount by which the pay-

Table 3.4

Summarized Income and Cost Rate and the Actual Balance of Combined OASI and DI Trust Funds for Future Income Periods (in percent)

Income period	Summarized income rate	Summarized cost rate	Actuarial balance
1997–2011 (15 years)	14.06	12.78	1.28
1997–2026 (30 years)	13.54	13.69	–0.15
1997–2041 (45 years)	13.42	14.66	–1.24
1997–2056 (60 years)	13.38	15.19	–1.81
1997–2071 (75 years)	13.37	15.60	–2.23

Source: 1997 Annual Report, Board of Trustees of the Federal Old-Age and Survivors Insurance and the Federal Disability Trust Funds (Washington, DC: U.S. Government Printing Office, 1997).

roll tax would have to be raised *now* (1997) to achieve an actuarial balance at the end of the seventy-five-year period. Note that this is smaller than the –6.07 percent shortfall found in Table 3.3 for 2075. The reason is this: if the payroll tax is increased *now* (1997) when there is an actual excess of tax revenue over benefits paid, not only will the assets in the OASI and DI trust funds be immediately increased, but the compounding of this increase through 2071 will bring the summarized income and cost rates into balance. These projections, of course, are sensitive to any changes in the underlying economic and demographic assumptions, a matter that will be discussed critically and carefully in Chapter 5.

At first glance, an increase in the payroll tax of 2.23 percentage points does not seem like an impossible economic or political change, although this represents a hefty 18 percent increase in the payroll tax. With this increase, the total payroll tax rate (employees and employers) for OASI and DI would equal 14.63 percent. One way to put such a change in perspective is to compare OASI and DI spending in 1997 as a percent of the GDP to the estimated value for this ratio in 2071. In 1997, the combined spending for OASI and DI was 4.7 percent of GDP; by 2071 this percentage

Table 3.5

Actuarial Balances* for OASDI and HI Trust Funds for Selected Years
(in percent)

Period	Combined OASI and DI balance	HI balance	Combined OASDI and HI balance
1997–2021	0.34	–2.10	–1.76
1997–2046	–1.45	–3.92	–5.37
1997–2071	–2.23	–5.05	–7.28

Source: The 1997 Annual Report, Board of Trustees of the Federal Old-Age and The Federal Survivors Insurance and Disability Trust Funds.
*Summarized income rate minus summarized cost rate.

will rise to 6.7 percent, a 42.6 percent increase in its relative share of the GDP.

If all that was needed was an increase in the payroll tax of this magnitude to secure the economic health of the Social Security system three quarters of the way through the next century, such a increase could be made politically feasible, especially if the increase was phased in gradually. But this doesn't take into account Medicare, which has a much more serious problem than the OASI and DI parts of Social Security. When this is done, the economic and political problems confronting Social Security become much more severe!

Factoring in Medicare

Since Part A (hospital insurance or HI) is financed by a 1.45 percent payroll tax,[12] the Trustees use the same technique used for OASI and DI for determining the actuarial balance in the HI Trust Fund, that is, they compare the summarized income and cost rates for specified periods. Table 3.5 shows the actuarial balance for the combined OASI and DI Trust Funds, the HI Trust Fund, and the combined balance for all the funds for three periods: twenty-five years, fifty years, and seventy-five years. The combined totals tell us how much current Social Security payroll taxes would have to be raised to achieve an actuarial balance for all three trust funds. These totals also provide us with a clear and decisive picture of the magnitude of the problem facing the Social Security system as the baby boomers enter the ranks of the retired. The figures in Table 3.5 represent a basic point of reference for the actions that need to be taken to achieve actuarial balance.

The worst-case scenario shown by the data in Table 3.5 is for the long-range period of 1997 through 2071, a seventy-five-year span. To achieve actuarial balance over this period, the combined payroll tax on the employee and employer for OASDI and HI (Part A of Medicare) of 15.3 percent would have to be raised *now* to 21.9 percent, which is nearly one-quarter of taxable wages and salaries, and a 43.1 percent tax increase. In terms of the GDP, spending for retirement and disability benefits plus hospitalization under Part A of Medicare would jump from 6.41 percent of GDP in 1997 to 11.64 percent in 2070, an 81.6 percent increase. By way of contrast, military spending in 1997 was 3.3 percent of the GDP.[13] It is hard to imagine *any* political circumstances in which such a drastic increase in payroll taxes could take place. Nonetheless, these are bottom line figures that spell out the magnitude of Social Security's problems in the twenty-first century.

Determination of Social Security Benefits

Now let us look at the other side of the coin, namely the benefits received under Social Security. Since Social Security is not like a private insurance annuity in which the income (i.e., benefits) depends on interest rates and the size of an accumulated fund, the benefits are determined in a different manner. Essentially, benefit determination under Social Security is an administrative process, in which past earnings play a major role with respect to the size of the benefits. The process itself is extremely complicated, but the general principles involved are readily understood.

First, there is the matter of eligibility. As noted earlier, 96 percent of people at work are in covered employment, which indicates that Social Security is a near-universal program. But this percentage, useful as it is, does not tell us precisely who is eligible for benefits under Social Security and Medicare. The basic principle—one that Franklin Roosevelt insisted upon to avoid Social Security having the stigma of a "dole"—is that eligibility for benefits is *earned* by payroll taxes paid by workers and their employers. This is fundamental. Currently, the basic requirement for benefit eligibility is the payment of Social Security taxes on a minimum amount of earnings for ten years; the minimum age for full eligibility is 65. Recent legislation increased the full retirement age, beginning in 2003 and gradually raising it until it reaches 67 in 2027. Workers who pay Social Security taxes for a minimum of forty quarters (ten years) are said to be "fully insured."

Currently, workers have the option of retiring and begin receiving benefits at the age of 62, although if they elect to do so they will receive only 80 percent of their full retirement. Benefits are adjusted accordingly for retirement between ages 62 and 65. Workers may also elect to work beyond the current retirement age of 65. If they do, their Social Security benefit will be increased, in part because of the extra income received for working beyond 65, and, second, through a special credit given to people who delay retirement. For persons who turned 65 in 1997, the increase was 5 percent a year. This rate gradually increases until it reaches 8 percent per year for persons turning age 65 in 2008.

Social Security is not just a retirement program. It also provides for disability benefits to workers and an array of benefits to members of a worker's family. Disability benefits under Social Security are defined strictly as a physical or mental impairment that keeps an individual from doing any "substantial work" for at least a year. Substantial work means monthly earnings of $500 or more. Disability benefits will continue unless an individual's condition improves, or the person is again able to perform substantial work. Actual disability payments vary widely, depending upon a person's age and earnings at the time the disability occurs, but are structured so that lower-income persons receive a higher percentage of their predisability wage than upper-income persons. For example, if a 45–year-old man with a wife and a child and a $20,000 annual income became disabled, he would receive an annual disability income of $14,568, or 72.4 percent of his prior income. If, however, his income was $50,000, he would receive $25,020 annually in disability benefits, or just 50.0 percent of his predisability income.[14] (See Appendix 1 for approximate monthly benefits by age and earnings.) Disability benefits as a percentage of earnings range from 72.8 percent for the youngest person with a spouse and child with the lowest annual income to 36.9 percent for the oldest person with a spouse and child with the highest annual income.

Social Security provides retirement and disability benefits not only for the primary wage earner in a family, but also for the spouse and children of the insured person. A husband or a wife is eligible for retirement and disability benefits if he or she is 62 years of age or older, or at any age if the husband or wife is caring for a child of the primary insured person, providing that the child is under age 16, or disabled. Children, too, are eligible for benefits if they are unmarried and under age 18; under age 19, but full-time students in a primary or secondary school; or age 18 and older, but severely disabled. Each family member is eligible for a monthly benefit up to 50 percent of the primary wage earner's retirement or disability income. There is a limit, however, to the amount that can be paid to a family, a limit that ranges between 150 to 180 percent of the benefits received by the primary wage earner. Divorced persons, even if remarried, may qualify for benefits on the record of their former spouse if they were married to the primary wage earner for at least ten years, are at least 62 years of age, are unmarried, and are not eligible for an equal or higher benefit on the basis of their own Social Security record. If an ex-spouse receives benefits, this does not affect the amount of the benefit paid to the primary wage earner or members of his or her family.

In 1994 there were 26.4 million retired workers (men and women) between the ages of 62 and 95 or older, who received an average monthly benefit of $697.30. Spouses of retired workers totaled 3.1 million, and received an average monthly benefit of $359.30, while children of retired workers eligible for benefits (under age 18 or disabled) numbered 440,000. Each child received an average monthly benefit of $309.10. Thus, a retired couple with one dependent child would receive an average Social Security monthly benefit of $1,365.70, or an annual income of $16,280.40.[15] In 1994, the poverty threshold for a family of three was $11,812, so a retired couple with one dependent child would have from Social Security an income above the poverty level.

Benefits payable to a spouse or children through Social Security are especially valuable when the family breadwinner becomes disabled or dies. In 1994, there were 4.0 million workers receiving an average monthly disability benefit of $661.70. Adding in their spouses and children gives a total of 5.7 million persons receiving Social Security benefits under the disability provisions of the Act. Spouses of disabled workers received an average monthly benefit of $159.70, and children an average benefit of $177.30. A married couple with one child and a disabled main breadwinner received $998.70 per month or $11,984.40 per year in disability benefits, an amount which would put the family just above the poverty line for a family of three.[16]

Finally, there are the benefits available to spouses and children of deceased workers. The spouse of a deceased worker got an average monthly benefit in 1994 of $655.70, and a surviving child under 18 or disabled if over 18 received $455.70 per month. In 1994 there were 5.1 million spouses of deceased workers and 1.9 million children, for a total of 7.0 million persons entitled to survivor's benefit under Social Security. Surviving spouses are overwhelmingly women, by a margin of 135 to 1! In 1964, a mother with one child under 18 would have received survivorship benefits equal to $1,111.40 per month or $13,336.80 per year, a sum comfortably in excess of the poverty threshold of $9,971.80 for a family of two.[17]

The disability and survivor benefits for members of a family provided by Social Security are extremely valuable. It would be extremely expensive for a family to purchase in the private market retirement and disability insurance of comparable value. In testimony before the Senate Finance Committee on March 11, 1996, Shirley Chater, U.S. Commissioner of Social Security, said that the disability protection provided by Social Security is equivalent to a $203,000 policy in the private sector, and Social Security's survivorship benefits are equivalent to a $295,000 life insurance policy.[18]

The benefit formula that underlies Social Security is based upon a worker's past earnings. The formula is designed to give low-wage workers a livable benefit in their retirement—this is known as the "social adequacy principle"—and also to provide a reasonable return on the taxes paid by all workers. The basic Social Security benefit—called the primary insurance amount (PIA)—is determined as follows:

1. The Social Security Administration selects the thirty-five highest years during which a retiring worker paid payroll taxes.
2. These earnings are indexed—that is, adjusted for inflation—to the year in which the worker turned 60. Earnings for years after 60 are not indexed.
3. The sum of the earnings—indexed and nonindexed—is divided by thirty-five to get average indexed annual wage, which in turn is divided by twelve to get the average indexed monthly earnings, denoted as AIME.
4. The benefit formula is applied against the AIME to get the worker's basic retirement benefit (PIA). Once a worker retires, his or her basic benefit is adjusted annually by the consumer price index to compensate for inflation.[19]

Table 3.6 shows the annual PIA for different levels of earnings for workers who retire at age 65 in 1998. The Replacement Rate is the annual benefit divided by the earnings in 1997. The benefit structure is inversely progressive; that is to say, lower-income

Table 3.6

Annual Retirement Benefits for a Single Worker Retiring at Age 65 in 1998

Earnings in 1997	Benefits	Replacement rate (%)
$20,000	$ 9,408	47.0
30,000	12,516	41.7
40,000	14,364	35.9
50,000	15,228	30.5
65,400	16,104	24.6

Source: Social Security Administration, *Understanding the Benefits,* 1998.

workers receive benefits that replace a higher proportion of their income than is the case for higher-income workers.

The progressive character of Social Security benefits offsets to a degree the common charge that payroll taxes are regressive. Actually, Social Security taxes are proportional up to their ceiling, which is currently $68,400. After that, Social Security taxes become regressive, since all employees with incomes above $68,400 pay the same amount of tax—$4,240.80. This amount becomes a smaller and smaller proportion of incomes above the ceiling, so in this sense the tax becomes regressive for very high wage and salary income.

Some light has been shed on these matters by a 1992 Commerce Department study of the effects of taxes and transfers upon the distribution of income and the percent of persons in poverty.[20] According to this study, in 1992 households in the lowest quintile (fifth) received 3.8 percent of total money income, while households in the top quintile got 46.8 percent of money income. Money income includes government transfers. If cash transfers from the government are removed, then the share of income received by households in the lowest quintile drops to 1.0 percent, while the share of income going to the top quintile jumps to 50.4 percent. Clearly, government transfers, which include Social Security benefits, reduce inequality in the distribution of household income.[21]

If we deduct Social Security payroll taxes and federal and state income taxes, but add in the earned income tax credit and non–means-tested government cash transfers, the share of income going to the bottom fifth climbs back to 3.8 percent, while the share going to the top quintile drops to 44.3 percent.[22] Thus, the distribution of after-tax household income becomes slightly less unequal as a result of Social Security and other non–means-tested cash transfers.

Another way to view the overall effects of Social Security is to look at the number of persons living in poverty[23] before and after the receipt of Social Security and other benefits. In 1992, the percent of people of all ages living in poverty on the basis of their money income was 13.1. If government cash transfers are deducted from income, then the poverty rate for all persons jumps to 21.2 percent.[24] For persons age 65 and older, the situation is much more dramatic. Without government cash transfers—overwhelmingly Social Security for the over-65 population—50.0 percent would be living in poverty. But when Social Security and other government cash transfers are factored in, the number of persons in poverty falls dramatically—to 12.9 percent![25] This figure is below the national average of 13.1 percent for persons living in poverty. For the nation's elderly, Social Security has been the single most important thing that has reduced poverty so drastically in their ranks.

Table 3.7 shows the sources of money income for family units age 65 or over by quintiles. As we move from the top quintile (fifth) to the bottom, Social Security becomes increasingly important as an income source. Families in the lowest quintile depend upon Social Security for 81.0 percent of their income, in contrast to families in the top fifth who get only 20.0 percent of their income from Social Security.

For all quintiles taken together, Social Security is of overwhelming importance, accounting for 57.3 percent of income. Property assets are next at 13.8 percent, followed by other pensions at 12.6 percent, earnings at 10.4 percent, and last, other sources, including SSI at 5.3 percent.

Table 3.7

Sources of Income for Family Units Aged 65 or Older by Quintiles
(in percent)

Income source	Lower fifth	Second fifth	Third fifth	Fourth fifth	Top fifth	Average
Social Security	81.0	77.3	61.8	46.2	20.0	57.3
Other Pension*	3.3	2.8	11.6	16.4	29.0	12.6
Earnings	2.6	7.8	6.5	10.6	27.1	10.5
Property Assets	0.1	6.4	16.7	23.9	21.9	13.8
Other*	12.9	5.6	3.3	2.8	2.0	5.3

Source: Social Security Administration, *Income of the Aged:* 1992.
*Includes supplemental security income.

Will the Social Security System Go Broke?

The last matter we want to consider in this chapter is the question in the title for this section, namely is the Social Security system going to go broke? This is the worry that is at the base of the expectations and fears of many baby boomers and others, although it is not always clear as to precisely what they mean by this. In the everyday usage of the term, "going broke" usually describes a business or household that can no longer pay its bills, an economic condition known as "bankruptcy." In what way can this idea be applied to Social Security?

The scenario posed by persons and groups fearful of Social Security's future health runs as follows. As already noted, the OASI and DI Trust Funds are currently running a surplus, which is invested in a special nonmarketable Treasury security, a Treasury IOU. The money, as we have also noted, flows into the Treasury where it becomes a part of the spending stream, indistinguishable from all other money that the Treasury receives. This is the major sore point with critics, giving rise to the outraged cry that they are "spending our money."[26] When around 2025 Social Security outgo (benefits) begins to exceed Social Security income (tax receipts), the Trust Funds will have to present these IOUs to the Treasury to get money to cover the deficit, the amount by which benefit payments exceed Social Security income. But the critics cry, the money isn't there, "the excess income or reserve in the Social Security Trust Fund has NOT BEEN SAVED. It has not been exchanged for gold reserves, nor invested in blue chip stocks, or real estate trusts. It is not even sitting in an account gathering dust. . . . *Instead, our government is quietly spending it!*"[27] The Treasury, not having the money to redeem the IOUs, will have to go to Congress and ask for money. "At this point, in plain English, the system is bankrupt."[28] To cope with the situation, Congress will have to raise taxes, cut benefits, or do both in order for the Treasury to pay the IOUs the Social Security Administration presents to it. What many fear, especially the baby boomers, is that Congress won't act to supply the money, but instead will cut benefits and allow the system simply to wither away.

That is the scenario seen and feared by Social Security's critics. Is it realistic? Is this Social Security's grim future? There is truth in the picture just drawn, but it is far from the whole truth about what lies ahead for Social Security. It is true that Board of Trustees projections show that Social Security income will begin to fall short of outgo around 2020, and that the combined OASI and DI Trust Funds will become exhausted in 2029. But it is not true that the Treasury IOUs that the funds hold are "worthless," as USA, Inc. maintains. Earlier in this chapter in the section "How Social Security Works," we pointed out that the Treasury IOUs that the Social Security Administration holds are, like all federal government obligations, backed by "the full faith and credit of the U.S. Government."

So for the Social Security system to go broke, the United States government itself would have to go broke, meaning that it could no longer collect taxes and that its debt obligations would no longer be honored anywhere in the world.

It is also true that, under current assumptions, taxes would have to be raised or benefits cut once benefits begin to exceed receipts and the Social Security Administration must cash in some of the Treasury IOUs it holds. This is not necessarily a catastrophic development that means the Social Security system is bankrupt. Rather, it is a signal that the system is facing serious, acute problems, beginning around 2020, but also that there is time—precious time—to begin working on solutions before it is too late. This is the real lesson to be drawn from woeful cries of groups that see Social Security as either bankrupt or heading in that direction. This lesson and the solutions it calls for will occupy us in Chapters 4 and 5 of this book.

— 4 —

Social Security and the Copernican Question

The problems confronting Social Security can be illuminated if we look at them from the point of view of what we shall call the Copernican question. This approach also leads us into the even broader issue of the role of "entitlements" in the American economy, since Social Security is one of the economy's most important entitlements.

The Copernican Question

For about 1,600 years (sixteen centuries) astronomers, mathematicians, and others interested in the solar system and the observation of heavenly bodies worked within the *Ptolemaic* system. Claudius Ptolemy (A.D. 127–151) was a Greek mathematician, astronomer, and geographer from Alexandria, Egypt, whose system of astronomy was based upon the assumption that the Earth was at the center of the universe. The observable planets and stars were presumed to rotate around the Earth, a view of the universe in harmony with the Christian doctrine of this era. In a practical sense for most of this long period, the Ptolemaic system worked quite well, especially for ocean navigation, which depends on the position of the stars in relation to the earth. Nevertheless, as time passed and as powers of observation increased, the system was confronted with an increasing number of anomalies, that is, deviations in observations that could be accounted for only by changes that made the underlying assumption less and less plausible.

At this point Nicolaus Copernicus, a Polish astronomer who lived from 1473 to 1543, enters the story. Essentially, what Copernicus did was *ask a different question!* What if, he is presumed to have said, we assume that the earth and planets revolve around the sun instead of the other way around? This was a revolutionary idea, especially upsetting to the Roman Catholic Church,[1] but one that explained better and more simply the actual observations that were being made with respect to the planets and other heavenly bodies. In science, the simpler theory that is in conformity with observed facts is generally assumed to be the better theory. What Copernicus did was, of course, unique and revolutionary, but in a sense all he did was ask a different question! Often a way out of a difficulty in a particular situation is to ask a *different* question, which is to say, look at the matter from a different perspective.

How, one may ask, does this apply to Social Security? What, in other words, is Social Security's Copernican question? The answer is this. The usual question posed in conjunction with the future of Social Security involves the number of expected workers per beneficiary. Since this number is forecast to decline significantly over the next seventy-five years, fewer and fewer workers will be required to support a growing number of retirees and other beneficiaries, a situation that may not only be economically difficult, but explosive politically. In the view of some, it is a situation ready-made for conflict, if not outright warfare, between the generations.

But what is the situation if, in Copernican fashion, we ask a different question? This different question involves the relationship between the expected number of workers and *all* dependents, not just retirees and other beneficiaries, but those at the other end of the age scale, namely children, young adults (mostly high school and college students), nonworking spouses, and others. This question puts the problems confronting Social Security in an entirely different light. The next sections explore these two crucial questions.

Covered Workers and Beneficiaries of the Social Security System

Table 4.1 contains data appropriate to the first point posed above, namely the average number of "covered" workers per OASDI beneficiary and the average number of beneficiaries for each 100 covered workers. Data are both historical and projected; both sets of data tell the same story.

That story in essence is the one feared by so many today—namely that fewer and fewer workers will be forced to support an ever-growing number of retirees and other beneficiaries of the Social Security system. In 1945, just ten years after Social Security began, there were 41.9 workers for each Social Security beneficiary—not a burdensome situation. Or to put the matter slightly different, there were in 1945 a mere 2.4 beneficiaries for every 100 covered workers. Covered workers in this context means workers who are in the Social Security system and who, of course, pay Social Security taxes. In 1945, the tax was only 1.0 percent on the employer and the employee, and it was for old age and survivors insurance only. Disability insurance did not become a part of the system until 1957.

From this point on, the situation has become progressively worse, at least from the particular perspective taken in the prior paragraph—that is, how many workers are available to support each Social Security beneficiary?

By 1995, the figures in Table 4.1 show that the number of covered workers per beneficiary had fallen to 3.3, or the number of beneficiaries for each 100 covered workers had climbed to 30.3.

The projected data show a continued worsening of this situation through 2075, when there will be only 1.8 projected workers for every OASDI beneficiary, or each 100 covered workers will have to support 55.6 beneficiaries. These numbers result from the fact that after 2010 the number of beneficiaries of the system

Table 4.1

OASDI Covered Workers and Beneficiaries for Selected Years: 1945–2075

Year	Covered Workers per OASDI Beneficiary	Beneficiaries per 100 Covered Workers
	Historical data	
1945	41.9	2.4
1950	16.5	6.1
1960	5.1	19.6
1970	3.7	27.0
1980	3.2	31.3
1990	3.4	29.4
1995	3.3	30.3
	Projected data	
2000	3.3	30.3
2010	3.0	33.3
2020	2.4	41.7
2030	2.0	50.0
2040	2.0	50.0
2050	2.0	50.0
2060	1.9	52.6
2070	1.8	55.6
2075	1.8	55.6

Source: 1997 Annual Report, Board of Trustees of the Federal Old-Age and Survivors Insurance and the Federal Disability Trust Funds.

increases much more rapidly than the number of workers. According to the Trustees this reflects the wave of baby boomers reaching retirement early in the next century plus a much slower growth in the labor force because of the impact of the baby bust following the baby-boomer population bulge.

Another set of numbers employed by the Social Security Trustees to analyze the system's future are "dependency" ratios. Two such ratios are shown in Table 4.2, namely the dependency ratio for the aged (persons over 65) and the dependency ratio for *all* beneficiaries of the system. Under the category of "Aged" in the table, the first column headed "Ratio" is the population over

Table 4.2

Dependency Ratios for Aged and Social Security Beneficiaries for Selected Years: 1950–2075

	Aged		Beneficiaries	
Year	Ratio[1]	Persons[2]	Ratio[3]	Covered workers[4]
		Historical data		
1950	0.138	7.2	.061	16.5
1960	0.173	5.8	.189	5.3
1970	0.185	5.4	.271	3.7
1980	0.195	5.1	.312	3.2
1990	0.209	4.8	.295	3.4
1995	0.214	4.7	.304	3.3
		Projected data		
2000	0.211	4.7	.307	3.3
2010	0.214	4.7	.338	3.0
2020	0.275	3.6	.416	2.4
2030	0.335	2.8	.488	2.0
2040	0.369	2.7	.503	2.0
2050	0.372	2.7	.513	1.9
2060	0.398	2.5	.536	1.9
2070	0.410	2.4	.550	1.8
2075	0.415	2.4	.558	1.8

Source: 1997 Annual Report, Board of Trustees of the Federal Old-Age and Survivors Insurance andthe Federal Disability Trust Funds.

[1]Population over 65 divided by population aged 20–64.

[2]The number of persons aged 20–64 for each person aged 65 and over.

[3]Beneficiaries divided by covered workers.

[4]The number of covered workers for each beneficiary.

65 divided by the population aged 20–64. The historical data cover selected years since 1950, while the projected data pertain to selected years from 2000 through 2075.

The numbers in this table offer another way of looking at the future problems of the system, defined initially by the data in Table 4.1. In 1950, the dependency ratio for the aged (persons over 65) was 0.138, which means that the aged were only 13.8

percent of the 20–64 population. The latter is the main population base for the labor force. By 2075, this ratio is expected to climb to 0.415, meaning that by that year the aged will equal 41.5 percent of all persons between 20 and 64. Imagine what our society will look like when the numbers of aged will be almost half as large as the number of people between the age of 20 and 64. It will be drastically different from society today!

Although this is not shown in Table 4.2, the Trustees also predict that by 2075, the number of people over 65 will be slightly larger than persons under 20; the over-65 cohort will equal 85.9 million compared to 85.6 million for persons under 20. In sharp contrast, in 1950 the aged equaled just 23.6 percent (12.7 million vs. 53.9 million) of persons 20 years of age and younger.[2] These are the demographics; behind them lies the picture of an America changing dramatically from a youth-oriented to an age-oriented society. In a sense in the next century, America will experience a boom in the aged comparable in its social and economic impact to the explosion of the baby boomers after World War II. One difference, though, is that we know the "senior boom" is coming, so the nation has more time to prepare for it than it did for the baby boom. As with the earlier baby boom, crucial aspects of our lives—the family, the nature of work, the character of leisure, the shape of education, the structure of production—will be transformed.

Returning to Table 4.2, the first column labeled "Persons" shows the average number of persons aged 20–64—the labor force base—for each person aged 65 and older. The numbers in this column are the reciprocal of the dependency ratio. This number declined from a comfortable 7.2 in 1950 to 4.7 in 1995. The really drastic changes are yet to come, as the projected data show it will fall to 2.4 by 2075, a decline comparable to the drop in covered workers per OASDI beneficiary shown in Table 4.1. The remaining figures under the heading "Beneficiaries" tell that same story in terms of beneficiaries and covered workers. In 1950 the dependency ratio for beneficiaries was 0.61, which means in that year persons over 65 totaled only 6.1 percent of workers in covered employment. As the last column in the table shows, there were 16.5 covered workers for each beneficiary, a number which is forecast to decline to 1.8 by 2075. By that same year, beneficiaries will climb to 55.8 percent of covered workers.

All these numbers tell essentially the same story: there is a serious number crunch facing Social Security in the future, as growth in the actual population of the aged (over 65) and all Social Security beneficiaries will run well ahead of growth in both the potential base for the labor force and actual numbers of persons in covered employment. The nagging political and economic question that worries so many is how will we find the economic resources and the political will to undertake the kind of massive transfer of income to such a large and growing, economically inactive segment of the nation's population envisaged by the numbers in these two tables? This gets us down to the nitty-gritty of Social Security's future problem—a transfer of income of an unprecedented magnitude. We must not lose sight of this perspective.

This brings us back to the Copernican question. What if we ask a different question? How will the problem appear if, instead of looking at the relationship between the workforce and the OASDI beneficiaries as in Tables 4.1 and 4.2, we ask what is the historical and projected relationship between the workforce and the *entire dependent population?* Would the problem then look different? Would any solution be easier? To these questions we now turn.

Table 4.3 contains the information needed to answer these questions. The table shows two sets of basic relationships for dependents. The first is between dependents and persons aged 20 to 64, and the second is between dependents and covered workers. From 1970 through 1995, covered workers averaged 85.4 percent of persons in the 20–64 age group, and for the period 2000 through 2075, the Trustees estimate covered workers will average 86.5 percent of the 20–64 age group. These percentages may strike some readers as relatively high, but the category "covered workers" includes people holding more than one job. This makes sense because a person holding more than one job will pay Social Security taxes in each job that he or she holds. For example, between 1960 and 1995, the average ratio of covered workers to employed workers was 113.5 percent, a statistic which is possible only if some workers hold more than one job.[3]

The other relevant statistic in this context is covered workers as a percent of persons aged 20–64, which, as noted earlier, is the population base for the economy's labor force. Between 1960 and 1995, covered workers averaged 85.4 percent of the 20–64 population; between 2000 and 2075, this ratio will increase slightly to 86.5 percent.[4] Again, multiple job-holding accounts for covered workers being such a high percentage of persons aged 20 to 64.

In contrast to the findings shown in Tables 4.1 and 4.2, the relationships in Table 4.3 show a significant degree of *relative* stability, both for the historical period from 1950 through 1995, and for the projected years from 2000 through 2075. To illustrate, the number of persons aged 20 to 64 for each dependent averaged 1.30 between 1950 and 1995. For the years 2000 through 2075, the projected average is almost identical, namely 1.31. Roughly the same holds true for the number of covered workers for each dependent, although the projected data show a slight increase—for the 1950–1995 period covered workers averaged 1.01 per dependent, but the ratio increased to 1.15 for the period 2000 through 2075.[5] This "increase" is a statistical quirk. As Table 4.3 shows, the number of covered workers per dependent was abnormally low in the years prior to 1980, a fact which lowered the average for the historical data as compared to the projected data. Actually, the Trustee's forecasts show that covered workers per dependent will decline from 1.41 in 2000 to 1.04 by 2075, a 26.2 percent drop. Nonetheless, we may note that the projected number of 1.04 covered workers for each dependent is larger than the comparable figure for 1950, 1960, and 1970. The number of covered workers per dependent is smaller than the number of persons between 20 and 64 per dependent, because covered workers are fewer in number than persons between the ages of 20 and 64.

Table 4.3

Dependency Ratios for *All* Dependents[1] for Selected Years: 1950–2075

	Population aged 20–64		Covered workers	
Year	Ratio[2]	Persons[3]	Ratio[4]	Covered workers[5]
		Historical data		
1950	0.719	1.39	1.380	0.72
1960	0.904	1.11	1.244	0.80
1970	0.898	1.11	1.091	0.92
1980	0.749	1.34	0.897	1.11
1990	0.700	1.42	0.801	1.25
1995	0.710	1.41	0.801	1.25
		Projected data		
2000	0.695	1.44	0.788	1.41
2010	0.652	1.53	0.752	1.33
2020	0.699	1.43	0.815	1.23
2030	0.788	1.27	0.906	1.10
2040	0.789	1.27	0.913	1.10
2050	0.787	1.27	0.918	1.09
2060	0.816	1.23	0.944	1.05
2070	0.825	1.21	0.957	1.04
2075	0.830	1.20	0.964	1.04

Source: 1997 Annual Report, Board of Trustees of the Federal Old-Age and Survivors Insurance and Disability Trust Funds.

[1]Dependents equal all persons over 65 years and less than 20 years of age. This understates total dependents because it does not include nonworking spouses between 20 and 64 years of age.

[2]Dependents as defined in (1) divided by persons aged 20 to 64.

[3]Number of persons age 20–64 for each dependent.

[4]Dependents divided by covered workers.

[5]Number of covered workers per dependent.

In spite of some fluctuations in the annual values for the relationships shown in Table 4.3, it is reasonable to conclude that the historic and projected links between the age 20-to-64 population and covered workers to *total dependents* is relatively stable, especially when compared to the pronounced trends shown in Tables 4.1 and 4.2. To put it differently, for the 125 years covered in these tables, the number of dependents in relation to the covered population has been remarkably stable! This is a finding of significant importance. What the numbers are saying, in other words, is that year in and year out, workers on average are responsible for roughly the same number of dependents. In economic terms, this means that a large part of the income workers earn as participants in the process of creating society's total income—the GDP—is transferred from them to dependents, both young and old. This is a bedrock fact that will figure in any solutions proposed for the problems Social Security will encounter in the next century.

The foregoing is fact number one—*all* dependents get their income through the transfer of income from the producing members of society. Fact number two concerns how this transfer comes about. The process is quite different for persons at each end of the age scale. As we have been discussing, the transfer process for the aged and the disabled and their survivors comes about through the mechanism of government—in the United States this is the Social Security system. The federal government collects taxes from the working population, and then uses this money to provide income in either cash or in kind to designated dependents—those eligible for Social Security benefits. For other dependents—mostly children, nonworking wives and older students—the process is quite different. Here the family is the key institution, for most of these transfers take place within the family. Intrafamily transfers are as old as the family itself, being underwritten by law in most societies. Parents, for example, are legally responsible for the support of their children and spouses. The payment of alimony when a husband and wife divorce is recognition of this. The important point, though, is that a transfer of income process takes place within the family, one that has been sanctioned by custom and law no doubt as long as the family has existed.

Prior to the emergence of social welfare legislation in the late nineteenth century in Western Europe and the twentieth century in the United States, nearly *all* transfers took place within the family. In the extended family characteristic of the nation's agricultural society of the nineteenth century, parents were responsible not only for the support of their children, but frequently for support of their own parents, once the latter could no longer work. The once-popular television program, "The Waltons," depicted this sort of a family. Most families in our modern society no longer fit this pattern.

How and why did this change? One of the risks persons face in the modern, industrialized economy is that of income loss when they face retirement, no longer able to participate in the economy as a member of the labor force. The bitter experience—especially during the Great Depression—of increasing numbers of persons in this situation convinced political leaders and citizens alike that change was needed. The result in the United States was passage of the Social Security Act in 1935. From the perspective that we have been following (i.e., that of the transfer-of-income process) the responsibility for the support of aged, disabled, and spouses of the aged was shifted from the family to the nation at large. In effect, what the nation did was to *socialize* the risk of an inadequate income in old age for most workers, relieving them of having to depend on their savings or their families for all their support once they no longer were full members of the labor force. The risk of insufficient income in old age has thus been shifted in part from the individual and the family to society as a whole. This is what is meant by the "socialization of risk." Americans shy away from talk of socialism and socialization, but the reality is that through Social Security and many welfare programs we are, in effect, socializing different kinds of risks or threats to income inherent in an advanced, industrialized society. Medicare in another example. Through Medicare, the nation socialized some of the threats to income caused by illness. What about youth and children at the other end of the age scale? Many European countries—and Canada—have moved partially toward socializing some of the cost of child rearing by children's allowances, payable to a family. The United States has not done this, although welfare payments (AFDC) offset some of the costs of child rearing for low income families.

The numbers in Table 4.3 show that the working population has been able—and will continue to be able—to support roughly the same number of dependents per worker. But, first, they do not reveal fully the demographic revolution that lies behind these data, and, second, they don't reveal either the fact that the problems associated with the future of Social Security are more political than economic. As to the demographic changes lying behind the figures in Table 4.3, they are astoundingly revolutionary.

We touched upon this earlier (p. 87), we need to underscore it again. In 1950, the over-65 population was less than one-fourth the under-20 population, 23.6 percent to be precise. By 1995, persons over 65 had increased to 43.3 percent of persons under 20. But by 2075, this figure will explode to 100.1 percent. In the years covered by this study, America is being transformed from a baby-boomer-dominated society to one dominated by the seniors—an aging society!

What are the political implications of this? They are obviously far-reaching, but one fact in particular has enormous political significance. In 1950, the greatest bulk of transfers—80.8 percent, specifically—took place within the household, an arrangement largely devoid of any political significance. By 2070, the statistics show that 50.1 percent of transfers to dependents will be directed to persons over the age of 65. This puts the political side of the transfer process clearly in the spotlight. Our existing body politic is able to manage through the political process the transfer of roughly one-fifth of all transfers to the senior population. But what will happen when this percentage share will have to be shifted drastically to provide benefits for the hordes of baby boomers who will begin and complete their retirement in the next century? Do we have adequate political machinery to meet this challenge? Can this shift be accomplished without an outbreak of generational war? These are some of the crucial questions which lie behind the figures of Table 4.3, questions to which we shall return to in Chapter 5.

A Larger Universe: Entitlements and Transfer Spending

At this point we need to broaden our analysis to include all transfer spending, including such spending that is characterized as "entitlements." The reason is that we cannot look at the problems confronting the Social Security system in isolation. They must be viewed in relation to the entire array of transfer spending that originates in the federal government. Further, any solutions to these problems will have to be worked out within this framework. It is also imperative that citizens understand the revolutionary change in the role and the functions of the federal government that has taken place in the half century since the end of World War II. First, though, we need to clarify the use of the term "entitlements," used increasingly to describe certain activities of the federal government since the end of World War II. Second, we need to show quite precisely how the growth of transfers and entitlements has changed the activities of the federal government in fundamental, even revolutionary, ways.

There is no precise definition for entitlements, although some economists define them as government payments that are paid automatically to individuals, payments to which they are legally entitled by virtue of age, prior employment conditions, or taxes paid. Typically, there is no means test in this definition. In the major entitlements such as Social Security benefits, unemployment compensation, Medicare, and pensions and disability payments for veterans and civilian employees of the federal government, the only role of Congress is to ensure that adequate funds are appropriated for these programs. As a matter of fact, a person entitled to benefits under any of these programs could sue the government if the benefits were not paid. Of course, since all these programs were created originally by Congress, the latter body has the power to alter or even abolish them if a majority so desired. This is highly unlikely with such long-established and popular programs as Social Security, unemployment compensation, or Medicare. The term "social insurance" is also used to described entitlements that fit this definition, which some would designate as the narrower of possible definitions for entitlements.

A broader definition would include programs generally thought of as "welfare," such as Aid to Families with Dependent Children (AFDC); food stamps; Medicaid; Supplemental Security Income (SSI), which provides aid to the blind, disabled, and aged (over 65) who do not receive benefits under Social Security; and the earned income tax credit.[6] These programs are usually described as "public assistance," because to receive benefits under them a person must be poor—there is a means test, in other words—and no prior taxes or contributions are required to be eligible. These are the programs the public generally associates with the word "welfare." Social Security, including unemployment insurance, and AFDC—originally ADC, or Aid to Dependent Children—were created during the New Deal, while Medicare and Medicaid were a part of President Johnson's "Great Society." The food stamp program came into being on an experimental basis under President Kennedy, but was subsequently expanded to become a major part of public assistance during the Nixon administration. The SSI program, which replaced earlier aid programs for the aged, the blind, and the disabled, was also enacted during the Nixon administration.

Senator J. Robert Kerrey, co-chairman of the 1995 Bipartisan Commission on Entitlement and Tax Reform, lumps all these foregoing programs together as entitlements. In addition to the above-mentioned programs, other programs such as benefits payable for black lung disease, aid to veterans, and low-income home energy assistance fall under the category of public assistance. Three other types of federal transfer expenditures are of major importance, but they do not fit into either of the above categories—that is, social insurance and public assistance. Nor is it appropriate to call them "entitlements." They are federal grants (called grants-in-aid) to state and local governments, interest on the federal debt, and federal subsidies to business.

Table 4.4 contains a breakdown of all federal expenditures for fiscal year 1997 by major categories of expenditures. The numbers in this table are especially instructive, particularly in view of widespread public ideas and misconceptions about how the federal government spends the nation's tax dollars.

Note, first, that slightly less than one-fourth (24.7 percent) of

Table 4.4

Federal Spending by Major Category: 1997 (billions of dollars and percent)

Category	Dollar value	Percent distribution*
Goods and services (G&S)		
1. Defense	$ 309	16.6
2. Nondefense	151	8.1
Transfers		
Social insurance		
1. Social Security	$ 362	19.4
2. Medicare	208	11.2
3. Unemployment Compensation	21	1.1
4. Other retirement and disability	81	4.5
5. Other[1]	37	2.0
6. Less: debt insurance	–14	–0.8
Total	$ 695	37.4
Public assistance		
1. AFDC	$ 17	0.9
2. SSI	27	1.5
3. Food Stamps	23	1.2
4. Medicaid	96	5.2
5. Earned Income Tax Credit	22	1.2
6. Other[2]	19	1.0
Total	$ 204	11.0
Interest on federal debt	244	13.1
Grants-in-aid	221	11.9
Subsidies	38	2.0
Total transfers	$1,402	75.4
Total Government Spending	$1,862	100.0

Source: Congressional Budget Office, *The Economic and Budget Outlook*, August 1998.

[1]Veterans' benefits, income and income supports, social services.

[2]Veterans' pensions, student loans, children's health and nutrition.

*Totals may not add to 100 because of rounding.

the federal government's spending was for goods and services, including the services of labor. The goods and services that the government buys in the marketplace constitute the resources which the government needs for all the commonplace activities people think of when they hear the word *government*—maintaining armies, navies, and air fleets; building and maintaining roads;

running school systems; operating court systems; delivering the mail; creating parks; providing fire and police protection; and other things that private business cannot do or would not be able to do on a scale adequate to the needs of society. If we want to measure the *size* of the federal government in relation to the production of goods and services by the private sector, we should calculate the purchases of goods and services by the federal government as a percent of the GDP. To illustrate, in 1997, federal spending for goods and services accounted for but 6.4 percent of the GDP; purchases of goods and services by *all* governments in the United States—federal, state, and local—was 17.8 percent of the GDP in 1997, so state and local government uses a larger share of the GDP than does the federal government.[7]

Buying goods and services to support its activities is only one of the two major things that the federal government does. The other, as we have been discussing throughout this book, is *to transfer income* from one part of the society to another. Technically, government expenditures that transfer income provide individuals, business firms, organizations, and even other units of government (federal grants-in aid) with income in either money or in-kind (like food stamps) for which the receiving entity is not required to provide a service, product, or money payment. Further, the receiving entity has no future obligation to repay the income. As the figures in Table 4.4 illustrate, the *transfer of income* has become the major activity of the federal government. In 1997, transfer expenditures accounted for 75.4 percent of all federal expenditures!

To whom or what were these transfers directed? Table 4.4 provides answers to this question. The largest share of transfers come under the Social Insurance heading—accounting for 37.4 percent of all federal spending in 1997—and of these expenditures, Social Security was the largest single item in the entire federal budget. In 1997, it amounted to 19.4 percent of federal spending. In the overall picture, interest on the federal debt was next in importance, amounting to 13.1 percent of all federal outlays. One of the most interesting statistics in the

Table 4.5

Federal Government Purchase of Goods and Services and Transfer Spending as a Percent of Total Federal Spending by Decades: 1950–1997 (in percent)

Period	Purchase of goods and services	Transfer spending
1950–1959	60.1	39.9
1960–1969	64.3	35.7
1970–1979	45.2	54.8
1980–1989	41.5	58.5
1990–1997	34.1	65.9

Source: Economic Report of the President, 1988, 1997.

table is that all forms of public assistance—"welfare" in the minds of many people—is only 11.0 percent of federal spending, smaller than all other categories except subsidies.

The figures in Table 4.4 are simply the most recent that reflect an enormous—even revolutionary—change that has been taking place for nearly half a century in the economic role of the federal government. The magnitude of this change is shown in Table 4.5, which shows by decade, since 1950, federal spending for goods and services compared to federal transfer spending as a percentage of total federal spending.

In the decade of the 1950s, almost two-thirds (60.1 percent) of federal spending was for goods and services, as compared to 39.9 percent for all transfers. In the 1960s, the relative share of goods and services spending rose (64.3 percent), primarily because of Vietnam War spending. Thereafter, the relative share of goods and services spending in the total picture declined, falling to an average of 34.1 percent in the 1990s. Transfer spending rose accordingly, and by the 1990s the situation was almost the exact opposite of what it was in the 1950s. This has been an explosive but little-noticed transformation in the role of the federal government in our society. What makes this change especially signifi-

Table 4.6

Federal Spending for Goods and Services and for Transfers as a Percent of GNP or GDP[1] for Selected Years: 1950–1997 (in percent)

Year	Federal spending for goods and services	Federal spending for transfers	Total federal spending
1950	6.6	7.7	14.3
1960	12.5	4.5	17.0
1970	11.2	9.0	20.2
1980	8.9	14.6	23.5
1990	8.8	12.7	21.5
1997	6.4	16.0	22.3

Source: Economic Report of the President, 1988, 1997.

[1]Gross National Product (GNP) in 1950 and Gross Domestic Product (GDP) in all other years.

cant is that transfer spending, in contrast to the buying of goods and services by the federal government, powerfully affects the distribution of income in the nation. Those who pay the taxes to support this aspect of federal spending have their incomes reduced, while those who benefit from the transfers—both in money and in kind—have theirs enhanced. It is as simple as that. To put the matter slightly differently, the major role of the federal government in our economic lives has become one of rearranging incomes, a fact that many applaud and many deplore.

The extent to which this has happened can be shown by another set of relatively simple statistics, showing for selected years, since 1950, goods and services spending and transfer spending as a percent of the GNP or GDP. These figures are in Table 4.6.

Goods and services spending was 6.6 percent of the GNP in 1950, rose to 12.5 percent in 1960, and since then has fallen back to 6.4 percent. As noted earlier, this percentage figure represents the share of the national output being used by the national government to provide the goods and services expected from our national government. Transfer spending tells a different story. Except for its dip to 4.5 percent of the GDP in 1960, transfer spending has risen steadily, reaching 16.0 percent of the GDP in

1970. Overall, federal spending climbed from 14.3 percent of the GNP in 1950 to 22.3 percent in 1997, an increase that is wholly a consequence of increased transfer spending.

At this point, one might wonder how these changes have affected the distribution of income in the United States. The most recent study on the effect of both taxes and transfers on the distribution of money income to households by the Bureau of the Census found that the distribution of market-based, after-tax income is much more unequal than the income distribution that exists after transfers.[8] Without government transfers, both in cash and in-kind, the lowest fifth of households received 1.0 percent of aggregate income, while the top fifth received 50.4 percent. After transfers, including the monetary value of Medicare and Medicaid, the share of income going to the bottom fifth rose to 4.9 percent, and the share of income received by the highest fifth declined to 43.3 percent. The Census Bureau also found that transfers of income, both in money and in kind, were much more effective than taxes in raising the incomes of persons at the bottom of the income ladder. There is no objective economic standard which says how equal or unequal the distribution of income should be in the modern economy, but studies like the one just cited show that overall transfer spending—of which Social Security is a major part—have, in fact, reduced income inequality in the United States.

Unfortunately, the most recent Census Bureau data shows an increase in inequality in the distribution of *money* income in the United States. If Medicare and Medicaid did not exist, the situation would be much worse.

The Kerrey-Danforth Bipartisan Commission on Entitlements

Discussion of the fundamental problems confronting the Social Security system and the broader environment of transfer spending which is their setting, would not be complete without a review of the findings and recommendations of the Kerrey-

Danforth Commission (henceforth called Kerrey-Danforth) on entitlements. Appointed by President Clinton in 1994, the thirty-two-member Commission undertook an extensive analysis of the role and impact of entitlements on the American economy. Its findings were made public in January 1995.[9]

In its report, Kerrey-Danforth classifies federal spending into three major categories; (1) entitlements, which include Social Security, Medicare, Medicaid, and the transfer spending discussed in the prior section; (2) net interest on the federal debt; and (3) discretionary spending, which includes defense, education, infrastructure, and all other spending. They assume a continuation of present policies with respect to each of these categories. By projecting present growth rates in the three major spending categories ahead into the next century, they reach the extremely gloomy conclusion that by 2012—a scant fourteen years into the future—entitlement spending and interest on the federal debt will consume *all* of federal revenues! By 2030, spending for Medicare, Medicaid, Social Security, and the federal retirement program alone will absorb all the tax revenues collected by the government, estimated at 19 percent of the GDP. Total entitlements will soar to an unprecedented level of 37 percent of the GDP![10] The projected growth in entitlements is clearly unsustainable, but members of the commission were unable to agree on a specific set of reforms. A basic menu of reforms on behalf of the commission was presented by the co-chairmen, Senators Kerrey and Danforth, while commission members Robert Greenstein, J. Alex McMillan, Peter G. Peterson, Alan K. Simpson, and Richard L. Trumka offered their own recommendations for reform. Overall, the commission members offered fifty-three specific proposals for entitlement changes and reforms. The major proposals are summarized in the following paragraphs under five major categories.[11]

1. *Congressional, Civil, and Military Retirement.* Proposals in this category would reduce congressional, federal civil service, and military benefits; increase the retirement age for civil servants; and put a cap on combined military and Social Security benefits for military retirees.

2. *Health Programs.* The sixteen reform proposals in this category include: (1) reduce federal subsidies to Medicare by premium increases for both Parts A and B; (2) change the tax treatment of Medicare benefits by treating benefits as individual income, and include the value of employer-paid health insurance as income; (3) offset the effects of population aging by gradually raising the eligibility age for Medicare to 70; (4) reduce Medicare payments to health providers (i.e., physicians and hospitals); and (4) increase the payroll tax for Medicare by 1 percent (one-half on employer and one-half on employee).

3. *Social Security.* For Social Security the recommended reforms are: (1) gradually raise the normal retirement age to 70, while retaining 62 as the early retirement age; (2) reduce the benefits to upper income persons by means-testing the benefit formula for upper- and middle-income persons and limiting cost-of-living (COLAs) for these persons; (3) provide a personal investment plan option for all workers in lieu of 1.5 percentage points of the payroll tax; (4) reduce spousal benefits for nonworking spouses, but not for surviving spouses; (5) index the benefit formula to the consumer price index (CPI), rather than average wages; (6) expand Social Security coverage to include all new state and local government employees; (7) tax 85 percent of benefits for all taxpayers; (8) increase the payroll tax by 1 percent (one-half on employer and one-half on employee); and (9) increase the maximum wage subject to the Social Security payroll tax so that 90 percent of all wages are subject to the tax for both employers and employees, and apply the employer portion of the tax to *all* wages.

4. *Comprehensive Benefit Reforms.* In this category, proposed reforms include: (1) revising the consumer price index (CPI) for a more accurate measure of inflation; (2) delay the indexing of entitlements for one year; (3) means test *all* entitlements for high-income persons (above $100,000 for individuals and $120,000 for couples); (4) broaden taxable income to include all entitlements; and (5) starting in the year 2000, put a cap on all entitlements other than Social Security, Medicare, and civil and military pensions.

5. *Reduce Tax Expenditures.* Tax expenditures are revenue losses that result from federal tax provisions that grant special tax relief designed to encourage certain types of behavior by taxpayers or to aid taxpayers in special circumstances.[12] They are the equivalent of a direct subsidy to a taxpayer, but they do not embody an actual outlay. Tax expenditures are a relatively new concept, but since the mid-1970s, the Committee on the Budget of the United States Senate published an annual listing of major tax expenditures and their impact on the federal budget. They are also described as "hidden subsidies," because they have the same effect as a direct subsidy, but because Congress does not enact them anew every year, they are hidden from the public view. In this category, the major recommendations of the Kerrey-Danforth Commission are: (1) starting in the year 2000, gradually reduce the home mortgage principal eligible for an interest deduction to $300,000; (2) eliminate the income tax deduction for state and local taxes, again to begin in 2000 and be phased in over a five-year period; (3) modify the deduction for charitable contributions to allow a deduction only if the amount exceeds 2 percent of a taxpayer's adjusted gross income; and (4) place a percentage limitation on the value of itemized deductions.

The most severe criticism of the commission's recommendation was by Commissioner Richard L. Trumka, president of the United Mine Workers of America, one of eight commission members who did not sign a letter transmitting the recommendations to the President. Trumka's basic criticism was that the report was one-sided, seeing solutions only through cuts in Social Security, Medicare, unemployment insurance, and programs for the poor, but neglecting to tackle the real budget issue, the exploding costs of health care. He is critical of plans to raise the retirement age to 70, claiming it would work real hardships on large numbers of older workers in poor health and with limited resources. Trumka also says that raising the Medicare eligibility age would be even more devastating, while the de facto consequence of the Kerrey-Danforth proposals would be cuts in Social Security benefits that would hit lower-income workers the hardest. He also asserts that there is no way in which the returns from "privatizing" a part of Social Security taxes could yield enough income to make up for these cuts. Women, Trumka says, would be especially hurt by these reform proposals. This is because women are more likely to be lower-income workers, they depend more heavily on their spouses for retirement income, and women live longer than their husbands.[13]

Peter G. Peterson did sign the letter of transmittal to the President, but he also submitted his own ten-point reform plan, one in which seven of the proposals were similar to those in the Kerry-Danforth document.[14] Peterson would enact a more comprehensive "affluence test" than in the Kerrey-Danforth plan, a test that would apply to all federal benefits, not just Social Security and Medicare. His test would be graduated and apply to all households with incomes above $40,000. In addition, he would enact a federal health care benefits budget, which would establish an annual budget for all federal health care spending with limits for each program. Peterson also would sharply cut back on agricultural assistance as a part of his comprehensive reform package, and depend increasingly on user fees to finance services that are now going to particular regions, businesses, and consumer groups, and are now financed by taxes.

The Unfunded Liabilities of the Social Security System

Before we turn to the discussion in Chapter 5 on the consideration of reforms and other actions that must be taken to insure the viability of Social Security well into the next century, we need to examine the issue of the system's "unfunded liabilities." This matter is a source of great worry and agitation by persons, like Peter G. Peterson, who fear the system is teetering toward bankruptcy. It deserves careful attention.

The unfunded liabilities of any kind of a pension or insurance scheme are the accumulated future obligations of a program that cannot be met from the earnings of a fund accumulated by contributions to that fund. In the case of private insurance, the premiums paid by a policyholder are the source of the funds. In the case of public pension schemes, like Social Security, any unfunded liability is the amount that future taxpayers are obligated to pay for the services already rendered by current and former workers.[15] Unfunded liabilities measure how far out of balance a system's existing assets and liabilities are. Herman B. Leonard calls this the "quiet side" of Social Security spending—the accrual of future liabilities to future recipients in the absence of funds to pay for them.[16] The actual spending is the change in the accrued liabilities that occurs from year to year. Professor Leonard argues that the unfunded liabilities of the Social Security system are not just an abstraction—they have been the engine for much of the program's expansion. They are a consequence of a pay-as-you-go system, which has been the basic nature of Social Security. It is relatively easy to expand a pay-as-you-go system because the added spending resulting from expansion lies in the future, as do the taxes needed to pay for the expansion. When the future arrives, members of the generation that engineered the increased benefits will believe they are entitled to the benefits because they have paid taxes into the system during their working lives.[17]

How large are the unfunded liabilities of the Social Security system? Their actual size depends on an array of variables whose future values can only be estimated, such as future rates of return on federal securities, the growth of the wage base for Social Security, the growth of the GDP, decisions about early retirement by members of the workforce, life-expectancy rates for retirees and other beneficiaries of the Social Security system, demographic changes that affect the working population, and others. Peter G. Peterson, a severe critic of the current system, claims that the unfunded liabilities of the federal government for both Social Security and federal pensions total $9.5 trillion, an amount 300 times the unfunded liabilities of all private pension plans in the United States.[18] Peterson scornfully calls these estimated future liabilities a "net gift that we are asking from taxpayers in future years to cover benefit promises that have already accrued in past years . . . ," one which will "have to be paid off, just like the publicly held national debt."[19] As for the trust funds, Peterson regards trust fund accounting as a hoax, and Social Security as a "vast Ponzi scheme in which only the first persons in are big winners and the vast array of those who join late in the game lose."[20]

Is Peterson correct? That depends in part on a clear understanding of the nature of the Social Security system, as well as the future health of the nation's economy. What Peterson is really lamenting is that Social Security is not a true "pay-for-yourself" system. A pay-for-yourself system is one in which each generation of retirees pays for its own benefits. It does this by the accumulation of a fund out of which benefits are paid when they come due. Such a system is said to be "fully funded" if at any one time it would be able to pay benefits without having to depend on new contributors entering into the system. A private insurance annuity is of this nature, as are most private pension plans.

In the debates within the Roosevelt administration leading up to the creation of Social Security in 1935, Roosevelt and his Secretary of the Treasury Henry Morgenthau, Jr., leaned heavily toward a pay-for-yourself system that would be fully funded, otherwise they feared it would not be "real" insurance. Secretary of Labor Frances Perkins, chair of the Committee on Economic Security, which designed the original plan, wanted a pay-as-you-go arrangement, but Roosevelt feared that this was just the dole under another name. Also there was worry that a fully funded system through a buildup of reserves might lead to federal ownership of large parts of the private sector. Nevertheless, the original legislation called for full funding, but the flirtation with full funding was short-lived. Amendments adopted in 1939 not only increased and extended benefits, but shifted the basis for benefits from contributions to wages, changes that made the system one of pay-as-you-go. This is the way Social Security has functioned until recently, when the build-up of large balances in the trust funds combined with talk of "privatizing" a part of the payroll tax has tilted some thinking about the system back toward a pay-for-yourself arrangement.

In their annual reports, the Trustees of the Social Security system have not shown any concern with the system's large unfunded future liabilities that are so worrisome to Peterson and others. They are concerned, though, with the financial adequacy of the system in both the short- and long-range. The test of the short-range (ten-year) financial adequacy of Social Security is having a trust fund ratio equal to at least 100 percent at the beginning of the period, and projected to remain at or above 100 percent throughout the projected period.[21] The trust fund ratio, the reader will recall, equals assets of a fund at the beginning of a period as a percentage of the outgo of funds during the period. As explained in Chapter 3, the long-range—up to seventy-five years—financial adequacy is measured by the "actuarial balance" of the fund, which is equal to the summarized income rate and summarized cost rate over the seventy-five-year period.[22]

Beyond these technical definitions of the adequacy and solvency of the Social Security system, the future health of the system—whether it will be there when the boomers retire in the next century—is the future state of health of the American economy. Social Security is a massive intergenerational transfer system, whose ultimate viability and durability depends upon the willingness of one generation to provide for the proceeding generations. No matter what the financial arrangements are, the bedrock economic truth is that some part of each year's actual output is being transferred through the system to persons in the population who are no longer economically productive. Future benefits can come only from future output, and if that output falters, or lags behind the claims on that output, serious difficulties lie ahead. Thus, the real key to the future viability of Social Security—and all transfers, for that matter—is the ability of the economy to sustain real growth. This, in turn, depends upon a number of other crucial variables, all of which we shall examine in our final chapter as we look at what must be done to keep the most popular social program ever enacted in the United States healthy.

— 5 —

How to Save Social Security

There is an aphorism that says, "If it ain't broke, don't fix it." That is the *current* situation for Social Security. There is no immediate crisis. The most recent (1998) reports of the Trustees for the OASI and DI trust funds state that it won't be until 2021 that outgo will exceed income, and not until 2032 will the assets for the combined funds be exhausted. These dates are better than those shown in the 1997 report, primarily because of the economy's recent better than expected performance.

The long-range picture is different, for the system will confront serious problems in the next century, first in approximately 2021 when expenses begin to exceed total income, including interest on trust fund assets, and more so in 2032 when the OASDI trust fund assets are exhausted. These problems are real, and they must be addressed, but, as stressed in Chapter 4, the nation has the luxury of time to cope with them.

For the baby boomers especially, the message is this. First, Social Security is not going to "go broke." Even in the worst-case scenario—that is, if nothing is done—tax revenues at current rates will be sufficient to finance 75 percent of benefits as presently authorized. But this need not happen, which brings us to a second point. It is the boomers, with their enormous numbers and potential political clout, who have the primary responsibility to forge the changes that will make certain that Social Security is fully viable not only for themselves, but for the generations to follow. Viability in this context must mean a level of real benefits comparable to what current beneficiaries now enjoy, not an austere 75 percent of the "normal" program.

An intense debate on Social Security's future is already under way, a debate whose scope and intensity can only increase as the nation moves toward the critical presidential election of 2000. At this writing in late 1998, a broad framework is emerging that puts the question of Social Security's future into two sharply different philosophic perspectives.

One aims to maintain Social Security essentially as it exists today, but finds within that perspective the necessary solutions for its future. The other is radically different, as it aims to change the nature of the system in a fundamental way. This is the drive to "privatize" the system, in whole or in part. These two vastly different "models" for reform are the approach we shall use in this book to answer the question of how we can "save Social Security." We begin with the highly controversial privatization vision.

The Privatization Thrust

"Privatization" is an awkward word, but one that has become fashionable in recent years. It comes from "private," as in private ownership, and in modern economic and political jargon means the ownership of something by an individual person or some nonpublic entity. It is the opposite of "socialization," which in a political and economic context means the shifting of ownership from the individual to a societal entity—a city, a county, a state, or the federal government.

Why has privatization emerged at this particular time as an important issue with respect to Social Security? Ronald Reagan, before becoming president, once mused that Social Security ought to be made private, but once he was president he dropped the subject. But it is back and back strongly in the political debate about Social Security's future that is now unfolding. Until after the "Big Fix" of the early 1980s, there was little talk of privatization in connection with Social Security. The reason was that generally the balances in the OASI and DI trust funds were just about equal to a year's benefits—the system was basically pay-as-you-go. Thus, any talk about privatizing the reserves did not make sense. But after the reforms of 1983, income began to exceed payments, with resulting large increases in the trust fund balances. The most recent report from the OASI and DI trust funds projects their joint surplus will reach a peak of $3,776.8 billion (almost $4 trillion) in 2020, before it begins a rapid decline as the baby boomers retire.[1]

During the last session of Congress, a number of privatization proposals were introduced, although none has yet emerged as law. Some would have the government invest all or part of the trust fund reserves in the stock market, while others would allow for the individual to own and control at least a part of the assets being accumulated from the payroll taxes. The latter is the distinguishing feature that would bring about a fundamental transformation in Social Security—changing it from pay-as-you-go to at least a partial pay-for-yourself system. What has made privatization especially attractive to many is the long bull market that began in the early 1980s, continuing virtually uninterrupted until the middle of 1998. Between 1981 and the end of 1996, stock prices in constant dollars as measured by the Dow Jones index rose by 257.3 percent, compared to a mere 48 percent for the nation's real GDP.[2] Corporate profits rose by 106.4 percent in the same period, which indicates that more than half of the gains in equity values during the latest bull market were speculative in nature.

The fact that in the recent boom long-term annual rate of return on equities (including appreciation) has been in the 7 to 8 percent range makes privatization attractive, especially for younger persons who are skeptical about the future of Social Security. What is overlooked is the fact that Social Security is not just a retirement program, but also it provides survivor benefits in the case of the death of a breadwinner, and disability payments when a wage earner can no longer work because of accident or illness.

Typical of privatization proposals is the bill introduced in March 1998 into the U.S. Senate by Senators J. Robert Kerrey

(NE) and Daniel P. Moynihan (NY), both Democrats.[3] Entitled the "Social Security Solvency Act of 1998," their bill contains eight major changes in the Social Security System: (1) beginning in 2001, reduce the combined OASI and DI payroll tax from 12.4 to 10.4 percent—by 2 percentage points—which would return the system to a pay-as-you-go basis; (2) allow each employee to invest the 2 percent cut in voluntary personal savings accounts, or, alternatively take the employee share of the tax cut as an increase in take-home-pay; (3) increase the Social Security Wage base to $97,500 by 2003; (4) reduce the cost-of-living adjustment by subtracting 1 percentage point from the consumer price index (CPI) used for this adjustment; (5) include all Social Security benefits in the gross income of the taxpayer; (6) include newly-hired state and local employees in the system; (7) increase the retirement age to 68 by 2017, and to 70 in 2065; and (8) eliminate an earnings test for individuals taking early retirement.

Two privatization plans, both more radical than the Kerrey-Moynihan scheme, are proposed by some members of the Advisory Council on Social Security.[4] The most radical of these would split Social Security into a two-tier system. The first—and lower—tier would establish a flat rate benefit for all persons eligible for Social Security. The second and much more far-reaching tier would involve a mandated Personal Security Account, to be financed by using 5 percentage points of the current payroll tax on employees. The Personal Security Accounts would be controlled by the individual worker. Enthusiastic supporters of this scheme claim that over a lifetime a worker who invested his or her 5 percentage points in the U.S. stock market at a real rate of return of 7.5 percent would end up with a retirement nest egg worth nearly $700,000.[5] The other proposal from some members of the Advisory Council is not so extreme. It calls for the creation of individual savings accounts, managed by the federal government, but financed by a 1.6 percent increase in the payroll tax paid *entirely* by the employees.

What is wrong with privatization, especially if the "magic of compound interest" is painted into the picture? As suggested above, advocates of privatization paint an exceptionally rosy picture of the returns that workers can expect from investment of some portion of the payroll taxes in the stock market. But these scenarios are based upon a number of questionable assumptions and an unwillingness to consider the disastrous social consequences that are likely to ensue if the nation goes down this path.

First—and foremost in the minds of many critics—is risk involved in investing a whole or a part of the current payroll tax in excess of benefits paid in private securities markets. These schemes are based almost entirely on the assumption that the recent bull market will continue more or less indefinitely into the future. While it is true that over the very long haul, the return on equities has been better than the return on government bonds or other investments, there is more long-term volatility in stocks than many people realize. As a matter of fact, very recent developments on Wall Street may have taken some of the steam out of the drive for privatization.

To illustrate, between July 17, when the Dow Jones average reached a high of 9337.97 for the 1990s bull market, and early October, this widely studied average dropped by 17.1 percent.[6] A worker nearing retirement at this time with a major part of his expected retirement income tied up in the stock market would be confronted with having to make a major downward adjustment in his or her retirement plans—or even postpone them. Or consider this. Between 1968 and 1974, the Dow Jones average lost 40.6 percent of its *real* (corrected for inflation) value! It was not until some time during 1989—twenty-one years later—that the real value of the Dow had climbed back to its 1968 level.[7] Mortimer B. Zuckerman, Editor-in-Chief of *U.S. News & World Report,* pointed out in a recent editorial that the stock market has posted declines about one-third of the time since 1900, declines that often last for fifteen or twenty years.[8] He says that looking at the long-term average rates for return on stock as a rationale for investing a part of the payroll tax in the stock market is comparable to a person drowning in a river whose average depth is four feet. There is also the matter of fees collected for the management of private accounts modeled after the popular 401(k) plans. These fees would be extremely lucrative for Wall Street, ranging up to as much as $136.3 billion by 2020.[9]

Another economist, John Mueller of Buell Mueller Cannon, Inc. notes that in this century there were three twenty-year periods in which real rates of return for stock were either negative, or less than 1 percent—1901–1922; 1928–1948; and 1962–1982. He finds these twenty-year intervals significant because most families can save for retirement only during the last two decades of their working lives. Thus, any family putting money into the stock market for retirement would be hit hard if the last two decades of their working lives corresponded with a twenty-year slump! Of course, there is no certainty that this pattern will continue in the future, but it represents a serious risk. Mueller argues that the risk of this is too high in comparison to the smaller but more certain real return from Social Security.[10] Mueller also notes that recent observations about the returns on equities derive from a period of strong economic growth, but if economic growth is expected to lag in the future—as the Social Security Trustees assume—then Social Security income and benefits will also lag.[11] In other words, Social Security is only as strong as the economy from whence its real support comes.

Like the privatization plans just described, most such schemes postulate individual or private retirement accounts over which the owners would have a high degree of control. The only alternative to this is to have the federal government invest some or most of the trust fund balances in equities, acting on behalf of all Social Security beneficiaries. Although this would eliminate the excessively high administrative costs associated with individual accounts,[12] doing this entails other risks. Early on, the reader will recall, the Roosevelt administration rejected the idea of the federal government investing any Social Security surplus in equities because it could lead to large-scale government ownership of big chunks of private industry—a kind of "stealth socialism." With the trust fund balances for OASI and DI expected to approach $3.8 trillion early in the next century, this danger is manyfold greater than in was in the mid-1930s. Further, if the federal government had such a large stake in the equity markets, the temptation to use these investments as leverage for political manipulation of the market would be well nigh irresistible.

Government investment of the trust fund balances in equity markets is not the way most advocates of privatization want to go. But if privatization takes the form of private accounts under individual control, there are certain to be losers as well as winners. It goes without saying that in any scheme based on individual accounts, the government would still have a major regulatory role to play, exercising control over the kinds of accounts that could be set up to prevent outright fraud and abuse. Strict government regulation of this sort could not—nor should it try to—prevent the normal ups and downs of the stock markets. But even in the best of circumstances, there will be losers, especially among low-income workers and other persons not experienced or sophisticated in the art of financial investment. What will happen to the losers when retirement time rolls around? The income from a truncated Social Security system will not be sufficient to compensate them for their losses, and if the number of "losers" outnumbers the "winners," a likely outcome in a slump in the stock market, the political pressures to bail out the losers would undoubtedly be enormous.

One of the arguments pushed by privatization advocates is that it will increase private savings, which they consider necessary for investment in the kinds of real capital that raise the productivity of the economy. The belief that the economy needs more saving is a favorite theme of conservatives, derived from classical economics, an argument that they push unceasingly. It is true that the personal saving rate—the percentage of personal income saved—has dropped sharply, falling to a low of 2.1 percent in 1996, as compared to an average of 6.9 percent in the 1980s.[13] Overall, though, there has been little change in the rate of *all* private savings, business as well as personal. In 1960, all private savings (business and personal) as a percent of the gross domestic product (GDP) was 15.5. This percentage rose to a peak of 18.5 in 1975, and then dropped back to 14.8 in 1995.[14] More to the point, investment in durable equipment—that is, machines—has shown practically no change since 1960. In the latter year, investment in machines as a percent of the GDP was 5.6 percent; it rose to a peak of 7.8 percent in 1980 and then fell back to 7.4 percent in 1995, a higher figure than in 1960.[15]

Businessmen invest in machines and other forms of real capital because they expect to produce more goods (and services) with that capital, goods they expect to sell for a profit. It is the expectation of profit that drives investment spending, not the availability of savings. In the modern market economy, most investment is financed initially by credit—primarily bank loans. Savings comes later, because investment spurs production, which leads to higher money incomes for people, and out of which will come the savings to match the investment spending. The foregoing reflects what is essentially a Keynesian view of how the economy works, namely, that investment spending, not savings, is the strategic determinant of output in the modern economy. In fact, privatization could readily compound the problem, for increased savings leads to less consumption spending, which in turn will depress the economy. This involves what Keynes called the "fallacy of composition," which says that what is good for the part may not be necessarily good for the whole. For any one individual, more savings may be a good thing, but an attempt by everyone to save more may not because it may depress consumption and output, leading to less saving for everyone.

One of the serious and adverse developments in the United States has been a worsening in recent decades in the distribution of income and wealth. From the middle years of the Great Depression until the early 1970s, both the distribution of income and wealth became less concentrated. For example, in 1936 the top fifth of families received 51.7 percent of money income, with just 4.1 percent going to the lowest fifth. By 1973, however, the share of the top fifth had dropped to 41.4 percent, as the lower fifth increased its share to 5.5 percent. But after 1973, this trend was reversed, with the upper fifth receiving 46.9 percent by the mid-1990s and the share of the lower fifth dropping back to 4.1 percent, about where it was in the mid-1930s.[16] The story is the same for the ownership of wealth. On the eve of the Great Depression, the top 1 percent of the population owned 36.3 percent of the nation's personal wealth. By 1945, this figure had dropped to 23.3 percent, but after that it began to rise again, reaching 37.0 percent at the beginning of the 1990s.[17]

An adverse consequence of this is a shrinking of the wage base for the Social Security system. This is because a less equal distribution of income means more income is being derived from property sources (rents, interest, and profits), and less from wages. Thus, taxable payrolls decline as a share of the GDP. In 1997, taxable payrolls were equal to 40.6 percent of the GDP. By 2075, the Trustees of the OASI and DI trust fund estimate that this percentage will have fallen to 35.1, a figure that foresees a continuing decline in wage and salaries relative to property as a source of income.[18] The Trustees attribute this trend to the increasing proportion of high wage earners—those whose wages exceed the taxable wage ceiling—in employment covered by Social Security, a trend which also reflects a growing inequality in wage income.[19]

How will privatization affect these trends? There is no precise answer to this question, but there is a strong possibility that privatization in the form of individual accounts controlled by their owners will make for greater inequality among Social Security beneficiaries, which in turn will affect the overall distribution of income. Such an outcome is likely because the more affluent account owners with their more sophisticated knowledge of equity markets will probably be more successful than the less affluent in their investments. To the extent this happens, it will offset the progressive structure of benefits that currently exists in Social Security. Even if the more affluent are not more successful in their investment strategies, reducing the share of payroll taxes that directly finances benefits will have the same effect. This is because only this share of payroll taxes can be used to structure benefits so that lower wage earners receive benefits that replace a higher proportion of their wages than do higher wage earners.

Perhaps the greatest danger from privatization is more intangible, not readily measured statistically. Now Social Security is strongly supported, even though it is in part an anti-poverty program, and it has a redistributional element in the way benefits are structured. What privatization schemes involving personal accounts may do is push us in the direction of a two-tier system, a low minimum benefit that increasingly becomes the major "safety net" for the elderly poor, and an upper tier in which the more successful and more affluent receive a greater share of the overall benefit package. Since the benefits paid by a reduced payroll that increasingly may be seen as "welfare," while other benefits are regarded as "earned," the solid support that now characterizes Social Security may disappear. This would be socially, economically, and politically divisive, hardly a desirable outcome. A Social Security house half social and half private probably cannot survive.

Reform Within the Existing Pay-As-You-Go Structure

The second broad avenue of reform seeks to retain the basic pay-as-you-go character of Social Security, but within this structure make the necessary changes to keep the system healthy well into the next century, particularly to meet the challenges posed when the baby boomers enter into retirement. As with the call for privatization, a large number of proposed reforms are already being intensely debated, and we can be sure as the nation and its economy move into the year 2000, the intensity and decibel count for this debate will continue to escalate.

Before turning to a review and analysis of the most important changes being proposed with Social Security's current framework, a brief review of the dimensions of the problems looming in the next century is in order. In Chapter 3, it will be recalled, we discussed the "actuarial deficit," which represented the amount by which the payroll tax would have to be raised *immediately* to bring income and outgo for the system into balance by 2075. For the combined OASI and DI trust funds, the Trustees now calculate this figure to be –2.19 percent, a slight reduction from the –2.23 figure they established in their 1997 report.[20] This, we noted, was a figure that was probably politically feasible, even though it represents a 14.3 percent increase in the current payroll tax. The rub here, though, is that these data do not take into account the hospital portion (HI) of Medicare. When this is factored in, the dimensions of the problem escalate sharply. For the HI trust fund, the latest estimate by the Trustees of the fund's actuarial balance is –2.54 percent.[21] When this is also added to the current rate (15.3 percent), the payroll tax would have to be raised by another 2.54 percentage points to a 20.03 percent rate (employee and employer combined), another 14.5 percent jump. This is not politically feasible, hence the search for solutions that can preserve Social Security without the necessity of such an extreme tax hike.

Within the existing Social Security framework, and given, too, the underlying assumptions of the Trustees' reports, there are two basic categories for reforms. These are (1) benefit reductions or (2) revenue increases. Within these two broad categories, a large array of proposals have been put on the table by a wide variety of interest groups. In the fall of 1998, with financing by the Pew Charitable Trusts, a Washington, D.C.–based organization, "Americans Discuss Social Security," put together a series of citizen-oriented forums in a number of cities across America to discuss and formulate proposals on not just the nature of Social Security, but its current and future problems, as well as what should be done to deal with these problems through legislation.[22] These forums will continue into 1999 and 2000, with the findings and conclusions of these citizen groups being sent to members of Congress in Washington. The format employed in these discussions is, in the author's judgment, well-chosen, and it will be used in the discussion to follow, but the judgments and conclusions that follow are those of the author.

Values and Social Security

The question of values is often one that strikes some people as smacking too much of "touchy-feely" sentimentality, yet it really cannot be avoided. Reasonable reforms of Social Security—as is true of any program for governmental reform—must rest upon a shared set of values. By this is meant an unwritten, but general, agreement within the society of why a program exists and what it is expected to accomplish. In the discussions and writings about Social Security, it is sometimes spoken of as a "generational contract," in which each generation pays for the retirement living of the previous generation, and, in turn, expects the succeeding generation to pay for its retirement. There is no law that expressly codifies such a "contract." Rather the "contract" is a widely shared social value whose concrete manifestation is in the existence and past support for treating Social Security on a pay-as-you-go basis. From this perspective, the campaign for privatization can be seen as an effort to modify this value—the social contract—in a fundamental way.

Another way of talking about the foregoing and similar values is to raise the question of "generational equity." In the abstract, there is little disagreement that Social Security in the way it works ought to be fair to each generation. To date, there seems to have been an acceptance (unwritten) of the view that, overall, the system is fair. But the emerging concern about the burden future workers may have to carry because of the fall in the number of workers per beneficiary of the system raises the question of generational equity. There is a fear that current demographic trends may place such a burden on future workers for support of the retired that they will rebel, giving rise to serious intergenerational conflict. Thus, intergenerational equity is an important value that must be taken into account and reflected in whatever action is recommended or taken.

There are other important values inherent in Social Security as it now exists, that must be preserved. Much of its popularity and political support stems from the widespread belief that beneficiaries are entitled to—or "deserve"—the benefits they receive because they have paid for them (at least in part) by the taxes paid into the system during their working lives. While this is partly a fiction in a strict economic cost-and-benefit sense, it is one of the important values that give the system such widespread popular support. This is why the efforts to introduce means testing into the benefit structure are so dangerous. Peter G. Peterson and others of like mind are offended that the wealthy receive benefits which a "means test" would disclose that they clearly do not need. To start down this path would endanger the unity that now exists, the belief that Social Security makes possible a life of dignity and independence for America's aged.

Another important value stressed in the "Americans Discuss Social Security" forums is preservation of the integrity of the system. What does this mean? Several developments underscore the importance of this, even though they don't explain fully what "integrity" in this context means.

One is the argument, discussed earlier, that organizations like TREA Senior Citizens League raise that "they are spending our money," or Peter G. Peterson's more sophisticated argument that Social Security is, in reality, a Ponzi scheme. The fact, too, that so many young people doubt Social Security's continued existence reflects a deep-seated doubt about the integrity of the system. To some extent, these things also reflect a growing distrust in the faith and honesty of the federal government, an unhappy development of our time. But, they also result from not fully understanding the essential nature of Social Security, how it really works. Thus, to maintain—and restore, where necessary—faith in the integrity of Social Security requires first that the workings of the system be fully understood. This is one of the goals of the "Americans Discuss Social Security" forums, for which the organization is to be commended. If people understand how the system works—why it has been essentially a pay-as-you-go arrangement up to now—this will in itself build faith in the system's integrity.

It is essential, too, that the safety net character of Social Security be maintained. In our society the aged now have one of the lowest poverty rates of any socioeconomic groups in American society, a result that has come about primarily because of Social Security. This is what maintaining an adequate safety net really means—providing levels of support sufficient not only to prevent any of the aged from falling into poverty, but also to enable them by adding their own resources to this social safety net to live in material decency and comfort in the last stages of their lives.

Finally, we should not forget that Social Security is more than a program that ensures an adequate income for people when they leave the workforce. It is also a program of *social insurance,* an arrangement through which society offers essential care for the disabled, the survivors of a family's breadwinner, and for orphans. Very few citizens could afford to purchase a private insurance annuity that would afford their families the same protection they are entitled to under Social Security.

Proposals to Reduce Benefits

Practically all of the fifteen or more major proposals (see listing in Appendix 3) in addition to the Kerrey-Moynihan plan to solve Social Security's problems contain one of more ideas aimed at reducing benefits. The major ones are discussed in the following paragraphs.

Raising the Retirement Age

To a degree, this change is already being implemented, for under current law, the retirement agc for full benefits is being gradually raised to 67. It is now 65. It won't be until 2027 that it is fully in effect, for in that year persons born in 1960 will be able to retire. People will still be able to take early retirement at 62, but the retirement benefit will be reduced. The primary argument for raising the retirement age is that since Social Security was enacted in 1935, life expectancy has risen from 63 to 76, and Americans generally are now in better health in old age than they were earlier. For this reason, some would propose eventually raising the retirement age to 70, although this is not now being considered in Congress. As noted earlier, the "magic" age of 65 for retirement was selected first by German Chancellor Otto von

Bismarck, when he introduced the first worker's retirement program in Germany in the late nineteenth century. On the debit side, critics argue that this would be hard on people whose jobs are physically demanding; persons partially disabled, but unable to receive retirement benefits; and persons who cannot find work because of age discrimination.

Reduce the Cost of Living Adjustment (the Social Security COLA)

This proposal really hinges on the controversy that has swirled around the consumer price index (CPI) in recent years. The Boskin Commission reported in 1996 that the CPI overstated increases in the cost of living by 1.1 percentage points. These findings have been disputed by other economists, but nonetheless, most reform proposals recommend, like the Kerrey-Moynihan plan, to reduce the CPI applied annually to protect Social Security benefits from inflation by 1 percent a year. The late Professor Robert Eisner of Northwestern University, a severe critic of this argument, pointed out that a 1 percent reduction in the CPI as applied to Social Security would reduce benefits by more than 10 percent over an average twenty-year retirement.[23] Overlooked, too, in this proposal to reduce benefits by making an adjustment for inflation, that few, if any, *private* pensions plans have any provision for inflation. Even if the inflation rate were only 2 percent a year, a retiree would lose one-fifth of the value of his or her income in twenty years. Professor Eisner also argued that Social Security benefits should be indexed to wages rather than prices. In this way, he said, retirees would share in rising wages because of growing productivity, but would also share in any sacrifices that might be necessary if higher prices for imports leave us with a lower real output.[24]

Reduce the Benefits for High-Income Beneficiaries

Peter G. Peterson is a strong advocate of this. He argues for an "affluence test," which would be applied to all households with an income over $40,000, and which would reduce benefits on a strongly progressive basis.[25] Essentially, this is a means test applied to Social Security benefits. It is certainly true that many highly affluent families have no strong economic need for social security benefits, but means testing is not the way to deal with this. No matter to whom or what income group it is applied, means testing is a degrading process, one that would undermine the broad support that Social Security now enjoys. It would also be a disincentive to save. The benefit schedule is already progressive, in that low-income wage earners receive a higher proportion of their wage as benefits than do upper-income persons. This progressivity could be increased. A better way to deal with this particular matter is to recapture the benefits received by the wealthy through progressivity in the federal income tax. This would be less divisive than means-testing benefits for the wealthy.

Increase the Number of Years for Determining Benefits from Thirty-five to Thirty-eight or Forty Years

The benefit a person receives under Social Security is based upon the thirty-five highest years of income during a person's working life. This approach, it is argued, would lead to only a slight reduction in future benefits, and would help the system toward future solvency without resort to a major increase in the Social Security tax. Workers who do not have thirty-eight to forty years of work would be hurt because the years of low or zero earnings would reduce their average benefit. This would be more likely to affect women, who often spend several years out of the workforce to raise children.

Reduce Benefits Across the Board

The argument for this is that all beneficiaries, irrespective of their economic circumstances, must share responsibility for strengthening the Social Security system. The difficulty with this, however, is that it would have an especially hard impact on low-income persons who must depend on Social Security for the bulk of their income during retirement. If used at all, it should be only as a last resort.

Proposals to Increase Social Security Revenues

The other side of the reform coin for Social Security aims at increasing revenues. The major proposals follow.

Increase the Payroll Tax Rates

This is the old standby, one usually resorted to in the past when Social Security needed more money. With OASI and DI combined taxes on the employer and employee equal to 12.4 percent, and another 1.45 percent added in for Medicare, Part A, the payroll tax now is now 15.3 percent. Earlier (page 72) we noted the payroll tax would have to be raised ultimately to 21.9 percent to bring the income and outgo for OASDI and HI (Medicare, Part A) into balance, an increase that is simply not politically feasible. For many low-income families, Social Security payroll taxes are far more onerous than the income tax. Further, the federal government gets an increasing share of its income from the payroll tax, which many critics regard as a regressive tax. For example, in 1960, Social Security taxes provided but 15.8 percent federal revenues, compared to 35.1 percent from the personal income tax. By 1997, Social Security taxes had climbed to 37.6 percent of federal revenues, much closer to the 44.7 percent supplied by the personal income tax. Corporate taxes declined during this period from 16.4 to 12.2 percent of federal revenues.[26]

Raise the Amount of Earnings Subject to the Social Security Payroll Tax

Currently the upper limit to taxable wages is $68,400. It is the fact that incomes above this limit are not subject to the Social Security tax that makes this tax regressive, when the actual tax paid is computed as the effective rate for *all* income levels. It is only the OASI and DI tax that is subject to the upper limit. To illustrate, a person with a $68,400 wage income and another person with a $100,000 wage income would each pay the same Social Security tax, $1,642 (rounded). The effective rate is 2.4 percent for the person with the ceiling income of $68,400, but the effective rate for the person with the $100,000 income is only 1.64 percent ($1,642 divided by $100,000)! As was noted earlier, taxable income as a percentage of total wage and salary income has been declining, a development that could be partially offset by raising the ceiling for the Social Security tax. The reason for a cap on wages and salaries subject to the Social Security tax is political, not economic. Currently, the taxable payroll makes up about 70 percent of the total wage and salary bill, so there is room to raise the ceiling.[27] Raising the ceiling will also increase benefits for upper-income wage and salary earners, but the increase will not be as great as the added revenue. All of any increase in the wage and salary ceiling will not be a base for any increase in revenue; since there is no ceiling on the Medicare, Part A tax (HI), this income is already taxed.

Economically, there is no reason why *all* wages and salaries should not be subject to the payroll tax; as a matter of fact, if the cap were eliminated, the tax rate for OASI and DI might be reduced, something that would be of great benefit to lower-income wage and salary workers. Politically, though, such a move would be strongly resisted by higher-income wage and salary workers, for their taxes would rise more than their benefits.

Cover All State and Local Government Employees by Social Security

This proposal would require that all *newly hired* employees join the Social Security system. Currently about 25 percent of state and local government employees are not in the system, an option that is exercised mostly by the employing governments. This measure would increase revenues immediately, but not costs until the employees begin to retire. If the intent is to make Social Security truly a universal system, there is little reason for this group of employees to remain outside the system. Currently, there are approximately 17 million state and local employees, so extending Social Security coverage to all these employees would over time bring a sizable number of new workers into the system. The transition costs would be troublesome for some states, notably Michigan and Ohio, where there is a relatively high concentration of these workers, but federal assistance could be provided to aid in this transition, particularly since the aim is to make Social Security a universal system. Probably, this is the least controversial of all reform proposals.

Tax Social Security Benefits like Private Pensions

Actually, the system has moved a long way toward this, as 85 percent of benefits above a threshold income—designed to protect low-income beneficiaries—are subject to the personal income tax. The proposition that *all* Social Security benefits ought to be treated as taxable income is more controversial. Given the drift toward increased income inequality in the United States, making all benefits a part of taxable income would not be desirable. Lower-income beneficiaries who depend heavily on Social Security benefits should be protected. Of course, if Social Security is their *sole* income source, they would not be subject to personal income taxes anyway.

An Alternative Approach to Solving the Social Security Problem

It is time to return to the "Copernican Question"—that is, to ask a different question. How will the situation look if we start from a different way of looking at the problem? All the proposals for change and reform discussed above rest on a set of assumptions about the economy's performance between now and 2075. These assumptions, as noted earlier, involve the rate of growth of real

Table 5.1

Real GNP, Population, Prices, and Labor Productivity for Selected Periods: 1839–1959 (in percent)

		Subperiods		
Category	1839–1959	1839–1879	1879–1919	1919–1959
GNP	3.66	4.31	3.72	2.97
GNP/Capital	1.64	1.55	1.78	1.64
Population	1.97	2.71	1.91	1.30
Prices	1.15	–0.16	1.19	1.40
	1889–1957	1889–1919	1919–1957	1945–1957
Productivity*	2.00	1.60	2.30	2.90

Source: Joint Economic Committee, Congress of the United States, *Staff Report on Employment Growth and Price Levels,* 1959.

*Weighted output per man-hour.

GDP, the labor force, the consumer price index (CPI), the unemployment rate, productivity, and other variables crucial to the economy's performance in the next century. The Trustees work from these assumptions to their conclusions about their impact on the Social Security system in the next century. We need to take a close look at these assumptions and their rationale, following which we shall examine how the problem looks from a different perspective.

In order to do this properly, we need, first, to look at past values for several critical variables. These offer guideposts for a better way to approach Social Security's problems, one that minimizes the laundry list of changes discussed in the previous section. Tables 5.1 and 5.2 contain these values. Table 5.1 looks at very long-term data on the performance of the American economy in terms of five key variables; real GNP, real GNP per capita, population, prices, and productivity. The data for the first four measures cover the 120–year period from 1839 to 1959, and for three 40–year subperiods within the long period: 1839–1879, 1879–1919, and 1919–1959. The numbers for productivity are

Table 5.2

Historic and Printed Growth Rates for Key Economic Variables: 1948–2075 (in percent)

Period	Current dollar: GDP	Constant dollar	CPI*	Labor force	Productivity**
1948–1973 (20 years)	7.05	3.69	2.68	1.55	2.12
1974–1997 (24 years)	7.65	2.53	5.49	1.77	0.86
1998–2075 (28 years)	4.78	1.59	3.41	0.41	1.18

Source: Economic Report of the President, 1988, 1997, 1998; *Annual Report*, Board of Trustees of the Federal Old-Age and Survivors Insurance and the Federal Disability Trust Funds, 1988.

*Customer Price Index.

**GNP or GDP in constant prices per employed person.

for different periods, namely overall from 1889 to 1997, and for three subperiods of different lengths, from 1889 to 1919, from 1919 through 1957, and from 1945–1957. There is some overlap between the last two periods. The productivity data were prepared by Solomon Fabricant, who in 1960 was director of Research of the National Bureau of Economic Research, and the other data by the staff of the Joint Economic Committee. The 1960 *Staff Report on Employment, Growth, and Price Levels* was one of the most comprehensive studies published up to that time of the long-term performance of the American economy.[28]

Table 5.2 contains another set of data that reflect the economy's more recent performance and projections through 2075. The figures in this table are for annual average rates of change in current-dollar and constant-dollar GDP (GDP has replaced GNP as the basic measure of the economy's performance), the consumer price index (CPI), the labor force, and worker productivity (GNP or GDP per employed workers). These two sets of relatively simple figures contained in these tables represent an enormous wealth of information, about not only where the economy has been, but where it is likely to go in the next century. Knowledge of the type and magnitude of changes awaiting us in these critical economic variables are extremely important for resolving Social Security's problems in the twenty-first century.

First, though, let us look briefly at the long-term performance of the American economy, a performance probably unmatched for such a long time by any other economy in the world. Overall, the nation's real output (GNP) grew over this 120–year period at a rate of 3.66 percent, a period that includes not only the Civil War, World Wars I and II, the Great Depression of the 1930s, and at least thirty cycles of measurable intensity since 1854.[29] So while America's overall material progress has been remarkable, it has been one of ups and downs—the familiar "business cycle." On average, periods of expansion have been about twice as long as periods of contraction—thirty-five months vs. eighteen months—which of course had to happen if the long-term rate of economic growth were to be positive.[30] The long-term cyclical performance of the American economy is one of its most important characteristics, although in the post–World War II period, periods of expansion have become much longer than periods of contraction, fifty months vs. eleven months.[31] At this writing (November 1998) the expansion that began in March 1991, has been under way for seven years and seven months, which makes it the longest peacetime expansion in our history, exceeded only by the 105–month expansion from February 1961, to November 1969, but this included the Vietnam War. So is the business cycle obsolete? Very unlikely. The question, though, is not irrelevant to our purposes, because the Trustees in their assumptions for their seventy-five-year projection period do not explicitly see any recessions. This is not surprising, simply because the ability of economics to predict any recession (or depression) with precision is practically zero. One might hazard the opinion that the low rate of growth foreseen by the Trustees in their reports through 2075 is a kind of hedge against the strong likelihood that there will be quite a few recessions between now and 2075. If we look at it this way, their lower forecast real growth rate for 1998 through 2075 than earlier periods (Table 5.2) fits in with the very long-term trend that shows our overall growth rate to be declining.

For the 120 years shown in Table 5.1 our annual rate of real growth per person (capita) has risen slowly, from 1.55 percent in 1839–1879 to 1.76 percent between 1879 and 1919, and then falling back to 1.64 from 1919 through 1959. The short but sharp depression of the early 1920s and the Great Depression of the 1930s were factors responsible for some slowing of this growth rate after 1919. Nonetheless, our nation's real standard of material well-being has been going up. Partly, this has happened because a fall in the overall rate of real GNP growth has been more than offset by declines in the rate of population growth. At an annual average rate of growth of 1.64 percent, real output per person would double in forty-two years. The assumptions found in the Trustees' reports indicate they expect the decline in population growth to continue, falling (even with immigration) to less than 1 percent annually as 2075 approaches. By the latter year, the Trustees assume labor force growth may fall as low as .1 percent a year—one-tenth of one percent![32] So even with sharply lower real growth rates for GDP, output per person will continue to rise, an outcome essential to a higher standard of living. It is interesting, too, to compare the historic long-term (1839–1959) performance of the American economy with respect to prices with the assumptions on prices made by the Trustees. From 1839 to 1959 (Table 5.1), the inflation rate—that is, price increases—averaged but 1.15 percent a year. For the next seventy-five years, the Trustees estimate consumer prices will rise at an annual rate of 3.41 percent a year.[33] This, though, is lower than our most recent experience (Table 5.2), when from 1974 to 1997, the CPI rose at an annual average rate of 5.49 percent per year.[34] These data may reflect the fact that our modern, complex world is far more inflation-prone than the simpler world of the nineteenth century.

The Copernican Question Again

Instead of *assuming* growth rates for GDP and other important variables as the Social Security Trustees do, let us ask a different question: what growth rate for real GDP *would be necessary* to

Table 5.3

Estimated OASDI and HI Income, Outgo, and Balance for Selected Years: 1998–2075 (in billions of current dollars)

Year	Income	Outgo	Balance	GDP
1998	$ 561	$ 524	$ 37	$ 8,384
2000	604	560	44	9,119
2010	980	991	–11	15,000
2020	1,583	1,967	–384	24,145
2030	2,504	3,671	–1,167	38,300
2040	3,984	6,103	–2,119	61,621
2050	6,251	9,725	–3,474	98,077
2060	9,776	15,733	–5,957	155,283
2070	15,281	25,423	–10,141	246,246
2075	19,073	32,252	–13,180	309,623

Source: 1998 Annual Report, Board of Trustees of the Federal Old-Age and Survivors Insurance and the Federal Disability Trust Funds.

bring Social Security revenues into line with forecast benefits? If such a rate can be determined, is it reasonable, in line with the economy's real potential?

Table 5.3 will aid in answering these questions, as it puts the coming Social Security problem in the most direct perspective possible. It shows for selected years between 1998 and 2075 forecast Social Security income (OASDI and HI), outgo, and the balance, plus GDP (all in current dollars). The income column excludes interest income on Treasury securities held by the Social Security administration, as this is essentially an intragovernment transfer. The income column then represents a precise estimate (by the Trustees) of what the *current* Social Security tax (including the taxation of benefits) will raise. This table includes data on Medicare, Part A (hospital insurance) but not Part B (medical services). Only Part A of Medicare is financed by the payroll tax. We will consider the impact of Medicare, Part B later. Income for Social Security of course depends on GDP and the Social Security tax, while benefits are determined by the eligible population plus the structure of Social Security benefits, matters discussed earlier.

The Trustees estimate that in 2075 the Social Security Tax (for OASDI) will be 12.4 percent, and taxation of benefits will be at a rate of 0.96 percent. Thus, the combined income rate will be 13.36 percent of taxable income, which is estimated to be 35.1 percent of the GDP.[35] Now we have all the information needed to determine the level of GDP that will yield Social Security Income equal to Social Security benefits in 2075.

Let us set up the problem as follows:

1. SSI = Social Security Income
2. SSI = SSBTX × SST × GDP
3. SSB = Social Security Benefits, including HI
4. SSBTX = Social Security Payroll and Benefits Tax Rate = 13.36%
5. SSTP = Taxable payroll as a percent of GDP = 35.1% (2075)

Solving for GDP:

6. SSI = GDP × (SSTP × SSBTX)

From which:

7. GDP = SSI/(SSTP × SSBTX)
8. GDP = $32,252 billion/(.351 × .1336) = $35,252 billion /(.0469). The $32,252 billion includes HI outgo, and is the amount of money needed to finance benefits in 2075, as shown in Table 5.3.
9. GDP = $687,675 billion, the required GDP in 2075 in current dollars necessary to yield a Social Security income equal to the forecast Social Security benefits in that year ($32,252 billion).

To reach this level of current-dollar GDP by 2075 will require an annual average rate of growth of 5.86 percent, starting from 1997 as the base year. We may call this our "required growth rate." This rate may be compared to the Trustees' current-dollar forecast growth rate for GDP of 4.78 percent, shown in Table 5.2. Now this current-dollar required growth rate must be translated into a growth rate for real output. The data in Table 5.2

shows that the Trustees' constant-dollar forecast real rate is 33.2 percent of its forecast current-dollar rate. So we shall use this percentage to convert our required current-dollar annual growth rate of 5.86 percent to the required growth rate for real output. This results in a required real output growth rate of 1.95 percent, a figure only 22.6 percent higher than the Trustees' forecast of a growth rate for real GDP of 1.59 percent! This is but a 0.36 percentage point change. In the light of the economy's historic performance (Table 5.1), including the economy's relatively poor performance from 1974 through 1997 (Table 5.2), this does not seem to be an impossibly large goal for the American economy. What is puzzling, perhaps, is why the Social Security Trustees set their sights so low.

Let us assume no change from 1997 to 2075 in the ratio of taxable income to the GDP. In 1997, this ratio was 40.9, but by the Trustees' estimates it was to decline to 35.1 percent in 2075, the ratio actually used in making the calculations in the prior paragraphs. Using the same formula with no change in the 40.9 ratio of taxable income to GDP, the required current dollar GDP would be $590,696 billion. It is lower because of the assumed no change in taxable income as a percent of GDP; thus, a smaller GDP will yield an inflow of SS tax income sufficient to support the forecast benefits in 2075 of $32,252 billion. This translates into a required annual average growth rate for GDP of 5.66 percent, which, using the same 33.5 percent figure as used above, gives us a required average annual growth rate of 1.89 percent for real GDP. This is 18.9 percent higher than the Trustees' rate forecast for real GDP shown in Table 5.2.

Let us try another assumption, which is that the ceiling on taxable wage and salary income for Social Security is raised sufficiently so that taxable wages equal 90 percent of the total wage and salary bill. Since 1960, wages and salaries have averaged 58 percent of the GDP, which means that taxable wage and salary income will be equal to $(.58 \times .90 \times .1336) = (.0697)$ percent of the GDP. Therefore, the equation will be GDP = $32,252/(.0697), or $462,725 billion. The required average annual rate of growth for current-dollar GDP is 5.83 percent, which translates into a 1.78 percent required annual growth rate in real GDP. This is but 11.99 percent greater than the Trustees' estimated rate.

What about productivity growth? By using the calculated figures for real GDP as determined in the preceding paragraphs, plus the estimated level of employment in 2075, it is relatively easy to compute values for output (GDP) per employed worker. From these calculations, we can get rates of growth for productivity between 1975 and 2015 under the different conditions assumed in the preceding paragraphs. To get the level of employed workers, we will use the Trustees' estimates of labor force growth and the unemployment rate.

On the basis of the Trustees' analysis, productivity (real GDP per employed worker) will grow at an annual average rate of 1.18 percent, significantly better than productivity growth from 1974 through 1997 (0.86 percent), but below that recorded from 1948 through 1973 (2.12 percent). For the alternative when Social Security income equals benefits and the taxable payroll drops to 35.1 percent of GDP by 2075, the calculated rate of growth of productivity will be 1.55 percent, a gain of 31.4 percent over the Trustees' 1997–2075 estimates, and 80.2 percent above the average recorded in 1974–1997. If taxable payroll does not drop to 35.1 percent—remaining at the 1997 level of 40.9 percent—then productivity growth will be 1.48 percent, which is still in excess of the Trustees' forecasts. Finally, if we assume that taxable wages are 52.5 percent of the GDP, then the calculated value for the annual productivity growth between 1998 and 2075 is 1.37 percent a year.

These projections for annual average rates of growth in current and real GDP and in worker productivity (real GDP per employed person) are summarized in Table 5.4. These figures help us bring the problems confronting the OASDI and HI parts of Social Security into a better perspective, including some possible ways in which the problem can be solved. Line 1 in Table 5.4 is the growth rates for real and nominal GDP found in the Trustees' 1998 report, and a calculated value of productivity growth from

Table 5.4

Projected Growth Rates for Real GDP and Productivity* Under Alternative Conditions: 1998–2075 (in percent)

Type or condition of protections	Real GDP	Worker productivity*	Current GDP
1. Trustees' protections	1.59	1.18	4.79
2. With taxable payroll at 35.1% of GDP	1.95	1.55	5.86
3. With taxable payroll at 40.9% of GDP	1.89	1.48	5.66
4. With taxable payroll at 52.5% of GDP	1.78	1.37	5.33

Sources: 1998 Annual Report, Board of Trustees of the Federal Old-Age and Survivors Insurance and the Federal Disability Trust Funds, 1988. Calculations by the author.

*Real GDP per employed worker.

data in the report. The Trustees assume a rate of growth for GDP for 1998 through 2075 and calculate the shortfall in Social Security income resulting from this approach—$13,180 billion as shown in Table 5.3. They are asking the question, "If the economy grows at a real rate of 1.59 percent through 2075, how large will the shortfall in Social Security revenues be?"

As noted several times, we are taking the Copernican approach—asking a different question. Our question is, "How rapidly must the real GDP grow between now at 2075 to provide Social Security with sufficient revenue to pay for benefits scheduled for that year?" Table 5.4 and the prior discussion shows three separate growth rates in answer to this question, depending on what is assumed about the size of the taxable payroll relative to the GDP. Each of these three rates is larger than the Trustees' projection, and each will cause enough growth in the real and current dollar GDP to bring Social Security tax receipts in line with benefits. The rate shown on line 2 has the same assumptions for taxable payroll as does the Trustees' projections, but the other two presume taxable payrolls as a larger percent of the GDP.

Four observations are in order at this point. First, as more of the total wage and salary bill becomes taxable payroll for Social

Security purposes, a smaller rate of future GDP growth is required to achieve balance in the OASI and DI accounts. Second, making a larger proportion of wages and salaries subject to Social Security taxes will lessen the regressivity of Social Security taxes, thus slightly easing inequality in the distribution of after-tax wage income. Third, the "required" rates of real wage growth are really quite modest, well within the economy's historic experience, even including the "Silent Depression" years after 1973.[36] Finally, we should note carefully, too, that the only "reform" required to reach a balance between OASDI and HI income and benefits is to expand the proportion of wage and salary income subject to Social Security taxes. No cuts in benefits are proposed, nor any increase in the retirement age beyond the one already scheduled.

The story is different when it comes to the productivity calculations. Here the picture is not so bright. Estimated productivity growth rates are below the 1948–1973 period (the "Age of Keynes"), as well as the long-term data shown in Table 5.1. In the long term (1839–1959), productivity grew the slowest between 1889 and 1919 (1.6 percent), a performance closest to the Trustees' estimates, but even this performance was ahead of the rates shown in Table 5.4. The lesson of these data is clear: improved productivity growth is an essential for dealing with tomorrow's Social Security problem. We shall return to this point shortly.

Factoring in Supplementary Medical Insurance

Now we can complete our analysis of the problem by bringing Supplementary Medical Insurance (Part B of Medicare) into the picture. Unlike Part A, Hospital Insurance, SMI is not financed by a payroll tax. Rather, it is funded by a premium paid by beneficiaries of SMI and general tax revenues. The Balanced Budget Act of 1997 provides that the monthly SMI premium be permanently set at a level that will yield income equal to 25 percent of SMI total expenditures. The balance of the funding will be through general appropriations by Congress.

Table 5.5 shows us the situation Social Security faces when

Table 5.5

Estimated OASDI, HI, and SMI Income, Outgo, and Balance as a Percent of GDP for Selected Years: 1998–2020 (in percent)

	Income				Outgo				
	OASDI	HI	SMI*	Total	OASDI	HI	SMI	Total	Balance
1998	5.19	1.50	.24	6.93	4.50	1.60	.97	7.23	–.30
2000	5.13	1.50	.27	6.90	4.53	1.61	1.07	7.21	–.31
2010	5.04	1.49	.42	6.95	4.83	1.78	1.67	8.28	–1.33
2020	5.03	1.51	.62	7.16	5.91	2.22	2.48	10.61	–3.45
2030	5.00	1.53	.77	7.30	6.79	2.79	3.06	12.52	–5.22
2040	4.94	1.53	.79	7.26	6.80	3.10	3.19	13.09	–5.83
2050	4.86	1.51	.78	7.24	6.73	3.19	3.10	13.02	–5.78
2060	4.79	1.50	.82	7.11	6.87	3.26	3.24	13.34	–6.23
2070	4.22	1.49	.83	7.04	6.92	3.41	3.31	13.64	–6.60
2075	4.68	1.48	.84	7.00	6.94	3.48	3.41	13.83	–6.89

Sources: 1998 Annual Report, Board of Trustees of the Federal Old-Age and Survivors Insurance and the Federal Disability Trust Funds; Board of Trustees, Federal Supplementary Medical Insurance Trust Fund.

*SMI (Premium Income). The Balanced Budget Act of 1997 (Public Law 105–33) set the SMI premium at 25 percent of program costs.

Medicare Part B is brought into the picture. It contains projected income and costs as a percent of the GDP for OASDI, HI, and SMI for selected years from 1998 through 2075. The SMI numbers reflect premium income only. Overall, the combined income totals for the three major parts of Social Security will rise from 6.93 percent of GDP to 7.00 percent in 2075, a minuscule 1.0 percent increase in revenues as a percent of GDP. On the cost side, the situation is drastically different, as combined outgo for OASDI, HI, and SMI jumps from 7.23 percent of GDP in 1998 to 13.83 percent in 2075, leaving the system with a negative balance of 6.89 percent.

What lies behind these projections by the Trustees is a slowing in the annual average rate of growth of the labor force, from 1.49 percent between 1945 and 1997 to a 0.41 percent annual rate between 1998 and 2075.[37] The primary reasons for this are the end of the baby boom, the lower birth rates for the "baby-bust generation" (1975–1985), a slowdown in the overall rate of labor participation rates after 2005, and a continued decline in the rate of participation in the labor force for men. From 1950 through 1985, the labor force as a percent of the population grew from 38.5 to 48.4 in 1985, then the growth leveled off, stabilizing at just over 50 percent.[38] This is the rate we use to estimate the population in 2075, given the above estimate of the growth rate for the labor force by the Trustees. On this basis, the labor force will reach 185.5 million and the population 371.1 million in 2075.

Since SMI income is not determined by the payroll tax, a different technique is required to estimate the size of and growth rates required for the GDP by 2075. An increase in OASDI, HI, and SMI outlays to 13.83 percent of the GDP (Trustees' estimates shown in Table 5.5) means almost a doubling of the relative importance of these expenditures in the GDP picture. Looking at the problem in this way, like looking at the expected decline in the ratio of workers to OASDI beneficiaries, suggests that the economy and its Social Security system is facing a truly formidable problem, one that calls for either drastic tax increases or a scaling back of benefits.

But there is another, more creative way to view the problem. If we factor in SMI benefits, using data from Tables 5.3 and 5.5, the total estimated outgo in 2075 for OASDI, HI, and SMI benefits will be $42,821 billion (in current dollars), instead of $32,252 as shown in Table 5.3. Using the same technique employed in the prior section, the GDP would have to grow to $913,028 billion by 2075 for a payroll tax of 13.36 percent to generate the revenue needed for estimated OASDI, HI, and SMI costs of $42,821. At this level of GDP, the total Social Security outgo in 2075 compared to the GDP will be the same as in 1998, 7.23 percent (Table 5.5). This, of course, is a considerable oversimplification, but it is not unrealistic. This GDP is almost three times greater than the GDP forecast by the Trustees (Table 5.3), but what makes this enormous difference is the power of compound interest. To reach a GDP of $913,028 billion (in current dollars), the economy would have to grow at an annual average rate of

6.24 percent. That translates into a real rate of growth of just 2.07 percent, certainly not an impossibility. Both of these rates, like those computed in the earlier section, are below the actual rates for both nominal and real growth from 1948 through 1997 (Table 5.2).

The Real Answer to the Social Security Problem

The foregoing statistical exercises point us in an entirely different direction—one which offers a far more satisfying answer to the looming problems of the Social Security System. This is to focus on economic growth, the ability of the economy to provide more real output for *all* the nation's citizens, including the beneficiaries of Social Security. In the coming debate over Social Security, we must not lose sight of the fact that Social Security is a transfer system, in which a part of the national output in any one year is transferred to the retired, the disabled, the survivors, and those eligible for Medicare. This is true irrespective of the financial means by which the transfer is brought about. There is no way under heaven to "store up" through savings a part of the nation's real output to meet the needs of those who retire, become widowed, disabled, or sick in the future. It must come out of future output, so that is why the growth of that output is so crucially important. And if it doesn't grow adequately? Then we are setting the stage for intergenerational class warfare—the young against the old, the old against the young! This is not a pleasant prospect.

And how do we get higher growth rates? The answer is through labor and the more effective use of our labor. The former, as we have already seen, is set as a result of deeply rooted forces now working themselves out—slower population growth, lower birth rates (the baby bust), and a leveling off of labor force participation rates. But the latter—the effective use of labor, or "productivity"—is not set in stone. It is something that is amenable to public policy. As Table 5.2 shows, the nation's productivity performance in the last quarter century (1974–1998) has been extremely poor, well below that of the Age of Keynes (1948–1973) and also its long-term historic average (Table 5.1). "Productivity," as Professor Paul Krugman of MIT has said, "isn't everything, but in the long run it is almost everything."[39]

So how do we increase the rate of productivity growth? There has been a slight revival in productivity growth, as in 1996 output per hour for all persons at work grew by 2.4 percent, and in 1997 by 1.2 percent.[40] This may be the start of a new uptick in productivity—but then again it may not be. In any event, the stakes are so great that we dare not leave such a vital measure to the vagaries of the market. So what is to be done?

There are many explanations for the decline in the productivity growth rate, not the least of which is "Military Keynesianism," the adverse effect of forty years of military spending on productivity.[41] None, though, are more important than those offered by David Alan Aschauer, Research Associate at the Levy Institute and Elmer W. Campbell Professor of Economics at Bates College in Maine. For more than a decade he has been conducting intensive empirical and theoretical research into the relationship between public investment and the nation's "infrastructure," and the relationship that this investment has to productivity and its growth.[42] Some of his main findings—findings especially relevant for the Social Security debate—may be summarized as follows:[43]

1. There is an important, strong, and measurable relationship between investment in public capital and productivity growth, a relationship he has carefully tracked since the 1950s.

2. The rate of public sector investment (infrastructure) has slipped from as high as a 5.4 annual rate in the early 1960s to 2.6 annually—or less—in the 1990s. Aschauer finds that as much as 60 percent of the drop-off in the annual rate of productivity growth in the 1970s and 1980s can be traced to the downturn in public investment spending.

3. The ratio of the stock of public capital to the stock of private capital that will maximize economic growth is approximately 61 percent—which is to say for every dollar's worth of private capital, the nation needs $0.61 worth of public capital. The actual ratio has fallen to 44.6 percent, or 26.9 percent below the growth-maximizing level.

4. Finally, the research indicates that a 1 percent increase in infrastructure spending will raise the national output by 0.24 percentage points.

The results of this research clearly point to the need for more public investment as the best and shortest way to raise productivity growth. Two critical questions remain: (1) how much public investment is needed? and (2) where would the money come from? There is, of course, no precise answer to the first question, but Felix Rohatyn, the distinguished New York investment banker, recently suggested that the federal government commit itself to spending $1 trillion over at least the next ten years for repair of the nation's infrastructure.[44] This would be around $100 billion per year, which in today's dollars would be 1.2 percent of the GDP—not an impossibly large figure. By comparison, military spending in 1997 was equal to 4.3 percent of the GDP.[45] Since a healthy infrastructure is absolutely essential to a healthy military, the $100 billion figure is not unreasonable.

The second question is more complicated: where would the money come from? The Kerrey-Moynihan proposal is to reducc the Social Security ratc by 2.0 percentage points and use the money diverted from Social Security taxes to investment in equitics—the partial privatization of the Social Security system. How much money would this proposal raise, either for equity or some other form of investment? Would it yield the $100 billion Rohatyn thinks is necessary to rebuild the nation's infrastructurc? Based on the income now being raised from the full Social Security tax in relation to taxable payrolls, the Kerrey-Moynihan proposal falls short.

Using data in the current *Trustees Report* for OASDI and HI, reducing the Social Security tax by 2.0 percentage points would free up an average of $38 billion over the next ten years for investment in either equities or the infrastructure. Taken by itself, an average of $91 billion becomes available from this move, but the lower Social Security tax leaves a deficit each year as income falls short of outgo. The saving for investment through the reduced tax must be offset by this deficit to get a true picture of the impact of such a cut on Social Security financing and the amount

Table 5.6

Social Security Income, Outgo, and the Effect of the Kerrey-Moynihan Proposals: 1998–2007 (in billions of dollars)

Year	1 Outgo	2 Trustees' income	3 Balance	4 K-M income*	5 Potential invest-ment	6 K-M deficit**	7 Actual avail-able
1998	$524	$561	$37	$486	$ 75	$–38	$37
1999	540	581	40	506	75	–34	41
2000	560	604	44	526	78	–34	44
2001	585	630	45	547	83	–38	45
2002	614	658	44	571	87	–43	44
2003	646	688	42	596	92	–50	42
2004	603	721	38	625	96	–58	38
2005	724	758	33	655	103	–69	34
2006	769	796	27	689	107	–80	27
2007	816	840	22	725	115	91	24
Aver-age	$646	$683	$37	$593	$ 91	$–54	$38

Sources: 1998 Annual Report, Board of Trustees, Federal Old-Age and Survivors Insurance, and the Federal Disability Trust Funds, and Board of Trustees, Federal Hospital Trust Fund.

*Amount of SS income with the Kerrey-Moynihan tax rate of 2.00 percentage points less than the current rate.

**Column 4 minus Column 1.

it might free up for other uses. Table 5.6 shows for the period 1998 through 2007 the effect of the Kerrey-Moynihan proposal on Social Security income and the potential savings for investment purposes.

One of the objectives of the Kerrey-Moynihan bill is to return Social Security to a pay-as-you-go basis, although as the numbers of Table 5.6 indicate the 2.00 percentage point cut in the Social Security tax goes beyond this. If, though, the proportion of wage and salary income subject to the Social Security tax were raised—as it should be—then it might be possible to reduce the Social Security tax more than 2.00 percentage points, and still raise sufficient income. As matters stand, overall the Social Security tax is regressive—this is because of the ceiling—and since it looms for many low-income families as important, or more important than the income tax, cutting the rate is highly desirable.

If cutting the Social Security tax rate does not free up sufficient funds for the $100 billion annual investment role, where is the balance of the money to come from, again without raising taxes? David Alan Aschauer suggests a possible answer. His research finds that only a small proportion of government spending is for investment spending, the bulk is for consumption such as military outlays, wages and salaries, and transfer payments.[46] The money is there, but getting it may not be so easy because the decisions involving government spending are made more for political than for economic reasons.

Assuming the $100 million can be obtained, the key question is how can a large-scale infrastructure investment program be organized efficiently, especially to avoid squandering the funds in pork-barrel politics and log-rolling business as usual? The answer to that is to develop a new investment institution, a National Development Bank. A new institution is needed, because the problem is not just reversing the decline in public investment that began in the 1970s, but also making certain that the future stock of public capital is adequate to the nation's needs. A National Development Bank could take the long view, alerting both the public and Congress to the nation's need for an adequate supply of public capital. Because about 85 percent of public capital is created and owned at the state and local level, the majority of decisions on spending for public capital should continue to be made at this level. But the funding will have to come from the federal government, hence the need for a new institution like a National Development Bank to guide these expenditures. Such a bank should make loans—not grants—to state and local governments. These loans should be low-interest, but not interest-free, and the states and local governments would be expected to amortize them just as they now do when bonds are issued to finance capital projects.

Aside from funds that might be released through a cut in the Social Security tax rate, there is no reason why a means could not be found to transfer some of the assets now tied up in the Social Security Trust Funds—the combined OASDI and HI Trust Funds will reach $3.8 trillion by 2020—into a National Development Bank. Putting some of these monies into an investment program for rebuilding the nation's infrastructure would be more productive than is currently the case. Further and to the extent that infrastructure investment enhances productivity—as it is clearly expected to do—more Social Security income will be generated, and thus a further lowering of the Social Security tax would be possible. All this is clearly contingent on an effective use of infrastructure investment funds, which simply underscores the need for a National Development Bank to mobilize and oversee the annual expenditure of a very large sum of money!

A Concluding Comment

The central theme of this book is that the nation's Social Security System, our proudest achievement in social policy, is facing problems, but it is in no danger of collapse. As a nation we have made a deep commitment to maintain the material well-being of the aged, the survivors of family breadwinners, persons disabled by illness or accident, and the health of the aged. The nation can and will honor these commitments. This is not to deny that there are serious problems facing the system, problems that must be resolved if the system is to continue to be viable in the twenty-first century. Fortunately, we have the luxury of time—time to contemplate, to prepare, and to put into effect solutions that will ensure this result. The most important lesson to be taken away from the analysis is the overwhelming importance of growth and productivity, the sparkplug for economic growth. Without economic growth, it won't be possible to maintain the system without drastic cuts in benefits, increases in taxes, or both. But with adequate growth in productivity and output, drastic measures won't be necessary, and a bitter intergenerational class war can be avoided. Productivity and growth—we must not take our eyes off this ball!

—— Appendix 1 ——

Economic and Demographic Assumptions

The following are historical data and assumed values for key economic variables for the calendar years 1960 through 2075. These are the data used by the Board of Trustees of the Federal Old-Age and Survivors Insurance and Disability Insurance Trust Funds. They are from the 1998 *Report* of the Board of Trustees.

Selected Economic Assumptions by Alternative, Calendar Years 1960–2075

	Average annual percentage change in:						
Calendar year	Real GDP	Average annual wage in covered employment	Consumer Price Index	Real wage differential[1] (%)	Average annual interest rate[2] (%)	Average annual unemployment rate (%)	Average annual percentage increase in labor force
Historical data:							
1960–64	4.6	3.4	1.2	2.2	3.7	5.7	1.3
1965–69	4.2	6.1	3.9	2.2	5.2	3.8	2.1
1970–74	3.4	6.6	6.2	.4	6.7	5.4	2.3
1975	–.4	6.7	9.1	–2.4	7.4	8.5	1.9
1976	5.4	8.5	5.7	2.8	7.1	7.7	2.4
1977	4.7	6.8	6.5	.3	7.1	7.1	2.9
1978	5.4	8.9	7.7	1.2	8.2	6.1	3.2
1979	2.8	10.1	11.4	–1.3	9.1	5.8	2.6
1980	–.3	9.4	13.4	–4.0	11.0	7.1	1.9
1981	2.3	9.7	10.3	–.5	13.3	7.6	1.6
1982	–2.1	6.4	6.0	.4	12.8	9.7	1.5
1983	4.0	5.0	3.0	2.0	11.0	9.6	1.2
1984	7.0	7.3	3.5	3.8	12.4	7.5	1.8
1985	3.6	4.7	3.5	1.2	10.8	7.2	1.7
1986	3.1	4.6	1.6	3.0	8.0	7.0	2.0
1987	2.9	4.6	3.6	1.0	8.4	6.2	1.7
1988	3.8	5.3	4.0	1.3	8.8	5.5	1.5
1989	3.4	3.9	4.8	–.9	8.7	5.3	1.7
1990	1.2	5.1	5.2	–.1	8.6	5.6	1.6
1991	–.9	3.0	4.1	–1.1	8.0	6.8	.4
1992	2.7	4.9	2.9	2.0	7.1	7.5	1.2

1993	2.3	1.9	2.8	–.9	6.1	6.9	.7
1994	3.5	3.5	2.5	1.0	7.1	6.1	1.3
1995	2.0	4.0	2.9	1.1	6.9	5.6	.9
1996	2.8	4.3	2.9	1.4	6.6	5.4	1.2
1997	3.8	4.5	2.3	2.2	6.6	4.9	1.7
1998	2.5	3.3	1.4	1.9	5.8	4.8	1.0
1999	2.0	3.4	2.4	1.0	5.4	5.0	.9
2000	2.0	3.8	2.6	1.3	5.6	5.3	1.0
2001	2.0	3.6	2.7	.9	5.9	5.5	1.0
2002	1.9	3.7	2.8	.9	6.0	5.7	.9
2003	1.9	4.1	3.1	1.0	6.1	5.8	.7
2004	1.9	4.4	3.2	1.2	6.2	5.9	.7
2005	1.9	4.4	3.4	1.0	6.3	5.9	.8
2006	2.0	4.4	3.5	.9	6.4	6.0	.9
2007	2.0	4.4	3.5	.9	6.3	6.0	.9
2010	1.8	4.5	3.5	1.0	6.3	6.0	.6
2020	1.3	4.4	3.5	.9	6.3	6.0	.1
2030	1.4	4.4	3.5	.9	6.3	6.0	.2
2040	1.4	4.4	3.5	.9	6.3	6.0	.2
2050	1.3	4.4	3.5	.9	6.3	6.0	.1
2060	1.3	4.4	3.5	.9	6.3	6.0	.1
2070	1.3	4.4	3.5	.9	6.3	6.0	.1
2075	1.2	4.4	3.5	.9	6.3	6.0	.1

[1]The difference between the percentage increases in the average annual wage in covered employment, and the average annual Consumer Price index.

[2]The average annual interest rate for the special Treasury obligations held by the trust funds for each twelve months of the year.

Selected Demographic Assumptions by Alternative, Calendar Years 1940–2075

Calendar year	Total fertility rate[1]	Age-sex-adjusted death rate (per 100,000)	Life expectancy[2]			
			At birth		At age 65	
			Male	Female	Male	Female
Historical data:						
1940	2.23	1,672.6	61.4	65.7	11.9	13.4
1945	2.42	1,488.6	62.9	68.4	12.6	14.4
1950	3.03	1,339.9	65.6	71.1	12.8	15.1
1955	3.50	1,243.0	66.7	72.8	13.1	15.6
1960	3.61	1,237.9	66.7	73.2	12.9	15.9
1965	2.88	1,210.8	66.8	73.8	12.9	16.3
1970	2.43	1,138.4	67.1	74.9	13.1	17.1
1975	1.77	1,020.9	68.7	76.6	13.7	18.0
1976	1.74	1,010.1	69.1	76.8	13.7	18.1
1977	1.79	981.8	69.4	77.2	13.9	18.3
1978	1.76	976.3	69.6	77.2	13.9	18.3
1979	1.82	944.8	70.0	77.7	14.2	18.6
1980	1.85	961.1	69.9	77.5	14.0	18.4
1981	1.83	934.5	70.4	77.9	14.2	18.6
1982	1.83	906.4	70.8	78.2	14.5	18.8
1983	1.81	916.0	70.9	78.1	14.3	18.6
1984	1.80	909.2	71.1	78.2	14.4	18.7
1985	1.84	912.3	71.1	78.2	14.4	18.6
1986	1.84	904.8	71.1	78.3	14.5	18.7
1987	1.87	895.6	71.3	78.4	14.6	18.7
1988	1.93	906.0	71.2	78.3	14.6	18.7
1989	2.01	882.4	71.5	78.6	14.8	18.9

1990	2.07	865.9	71.8	78.9	15.0	19.0
1991	2.07	854.8	71.9	79.0	15.1	19.1
1992	2.06	843.6	72.2	79.2	15.2	19.2
1993	2.04	863.3	72.0	78.9	15.1	19.0
1994	2.04	852.2	72.2	79.0	15.3	19.0
1995	2.02	849.8	72.4	79.0	15.3	19.0
1996[4]	2.03	821.8	73.0	79.2	15.8	19.1
1997[4]	2.03	823.4	72.9	79.3	15.6	19.2
1998	2.02	815.9	73.1	79.4	15.7	19.2
2000	2.01	801.5	73.5	79.6	15.8	19.3
2005	1.99	771.0	74.3	80.1	16.1	19.4
2010	1.96	749.2	74.9	80.4	16.3	19.5
2015	1.94	728.0	75.4	80.7	16.5	19.7
2020	1.91	706.7	75.7	81.1	16.7	19.9
2025	1.90	686.2	76.1	81.4	16.9	20.1
2030	1.90	666.7	76.5	81.7	17.1	20.4
2035	1.90	648.1	76.8	82.0	17.3	20.6
2040	1.90	630.5	77.2	82.3	17.5	20.8
2045	1.90	613.7	77.5	82.6	17.7	21.0
2050	1.90	597.7	77.8	82.9	17.9	21.2
2055	1.90	582.4	78.1	83.2	18.1	21.4
2060	1.90	567.8	78.4	83.4	18.3	21.6
2065	1.90	554.0	78.7	83.7	18.5	21.8
2070	1.90	540.7	79.0	84.0	18.7	22.0
2075	1.90	528.0	79.3	84.2	18.8	22.2

[1]The average number of children who would be born to a woman in her lifetime if she were to experience the birth rates observed for women of her age during her childbearing period.

[2]The average number of years of life remaining for a person if that person were to experience the death rates by age for persons of live age in each selected year.

Approximate Monthly Benefits if You Become Disabled in 1998 and Had Steady Earnings

		Your Earnings in 1997				
Your age	Your family	$20,000	$30,000	$40,000	$50,000	$65,400 or More[1]
25	You	$ 809	$1,076	$1,265	$1,390	$1,566
	You, your spouse and child[2]	1,214	1,614	1,897	2,085	2,349
35	You	809	1,076	1,265	1,390	1,559
	You, your spouse and child[2]	1,214	1,614	1,897	2,085	2,338
45	You	809	1,076	1,265	1,390	1,528
	You, your spouse and child[2]	1,214	1,614	1,897	2,085	2,293
55	You	809	1,076	1,257	1,348	1,442
	You, your spouse and child[2]	1,214	1,614	1,886	2,023	2,164
64	You	783	1,041	1,195	1,266	1,340
	You, your spouse and child[2]	1,174	1,562	1,793	1,900	2,010

[1]Earnings equal to or greater than the OASDI wage base from age 22 through 1997.
[2]Equals the maximum family benefit.
Note: The accuracy of these estimates depends on the pattern of your earnings in prior years.

—— Appendix 2 ——

The "Notch Babies"

The "notch babies" are persons born between 1917 and 1921, who generally receive lower Social Security benefits than those born before 1917. Before 1972, Congress adjusted Social Security benefits on an ad hoc basis. The 1972 Amendments to the Social Security Act changed the benefit formula to provide for automatic cost-of-living changes. But the method employed when combined with prices rising faster than wages caused future retirees' benefits to be overindexed—that is, benefits increased faster than the rate of inflation.

In 1977 the Social Security Act was again amended to eliminated overindexing and stabilize replacement rates—the portion of a person's pre-retirement earnings that the retirement benefit replaces. The new formula applied to persons born after 1921. Persons born between 1917 and through 1921 are known as the "transitional group," and their benefits were computed by using a transitional formula and the new formula, and because their benefits are still lower than for persons born before 1917, they have become known as the "notch" group or babies.

A lobbying group, TREA Senior Citizens League is pressuring Congress for a lump sum notch settlement of $5,000 for each eligible Social Security beneficiary born from 1917 through 1921. A notch settlement bill has been introduced into the House of Representatives United States Congress.

— Appendix 3 —

Social Security Reform Proposals

The following are the major proposals offered by various persons for reform of the Social Security System.

HENRY AARON
Senior Fellow, Brookings Institution

INVESTING THE TRUST FUNDS: A contingency reserve equal to 150 percent of annual benefits would be invested in government securities. Above this reserve, further accumulation would be invested to produce a fund consisting of half common stocks and half bonds (government and private).

BENEFITS: Social Security benefits would be taxed like contributory private pension income.

RETIREMENT AGE: The age at which unreduced benefits are paid would be gradually increased to 67 by 2012. The Early Retirement Age (ERA) would be increased to 64 by 2012. Both would be indexed to life expectancy thereafter.

COMPUTATION YEARS: The number of years used for calculating retirement benefits, now thirty-five, would be increased to thirty-eight.

STATE AND LOCAL WORKERS: Beginning January 1, 2000, all newly hired state and local workers would be covered under the Social Security System.

SPOUSAL BENEFITS: Spousal benefits would be gradually reduced from 50 percent to 33.5 percent. Surviving spousal benefits would be increased to 75 percent of the couple's combined benefit amount.

REP. BILL ARCHER (R-TX) H.R. 3546

Approved by the House on April 29.

A bipartisan commission of eight members would propose long-term reforms to keep Social Security solvent.

President Clinton would appoint two members, and Senate Majority Leader Trent Lott (R-MS) would select four members. Senate Minority Leader Tom Daschle (D-SD) and House Minority Leader Richard Gephardt (D-MO) would each select two members.

Final recommendations would have to be endorsed by at least six members of the commission.

PRESIDENT BILL CLINTON

The program is called "Save Social Security First." The budget surpluses would not be used, for either tax reductions or spending programs, until Social Security's solvency is assured.

A national debate and conversation about Social Security will take place during 1998. The president or vice president will participate in four town hall meetings, where citizens will discuss Social Security.

A special White House conference on Social Security will be held in December.

Early in 1999, the president will meet with congressional leaders to develop a bipartisan plan for Social Security's fiscal future.

ROBERT M. BALL

Former Commissioner, Social Security Administration

INVESTING THE TRUST FUNDS: Up to 50 percent of the Trust Funds would be invested in broadly indexed equities, phased in between 2000 and 2014. An amount equal to at least 150 percent of annual benefits would always be invested in government securities. A Federal Reserve-type board would be created to select the index, select experienced portfolio managers, and report to the public about the overall operation. Social Security would not have stock voting rights.

INDIVIDUAL ACCOUNTS: Beginning in the year 2000, voluntary supplemental individual savings accounts would be established. Workers would be allowed to have an additional 2 percent of their earnings, covered by the Social Security maximum earnings base, deducted by their employer. Workers would choose to invest the funds in Social Security's portfolio, or a 50–50 split between stocks and bonds.

COST-OF-LIVING ADJUSTMENTS: Cost-of-living adjustments would reflect corrections to the Consumer Price Index (CPI) expected to be made by the Bureau of Labor Statistics.

STATE AND LOCAL WORKERS: All newly hired state and local workers would be covered under the Sociam Security System effective 10 years after enactment of federal legislation.

WAGE BASE: The maximum earnings base, currently 85 percent of earnings in covered employment, would be raised 5 percentage points to 90 percent in the years 2000 through 2010.

EDWARD GRAMLICH

Governor, Federal Reserve Board

INDIVIDUAL ACCOUNTS: Individual savings accounts would be created in addition to existing Social Security benefits. Workers would be required to contribute an extra 1.6 percent of earnings to the newly created account. The contributions would be centrally managed and invested in five to ten broad-based index funds.

RETIREMENT AGE: The eligibility age for normal retirement would be increased from 65 to 67 by the year 2011, and indexed to life expectancy thereafter.

BENEFITS: The 32 percent and 15 percent bend point factors*

*The bend point factors refer to the percentages in the benefit formula used to compute Social Security benefits.

would be gradually reduced to 22.4 and 10.5 percent, respectively. The special income-tax exemption on Social Security benefits would be eliminated.

COMPUTATION YEARS: The benefit computation period would be extended from thirty-five to thirty-eight over a two-year period.

SPOUSAL BENEFITS: Phased in over time, aged spousal benefits would be gradually reduced from 50 percent to 33 percent, and benefits for surviving spouses would increase to 75 percent.

STATE AND LOCAL COVERAGE: Social Security coverage would be extended to all newly hired state and local workers.

SEN. PHIL GRAMM (R-TX)
SEN. PETE DOMENICI (R-NM)

INDIVIDUAL ACCOUNTS: Workers would place 3 percentage points of the payroll tax in a Social Security Individual Investment Account (SI). The money would go into investments regulated and certified for safety by a newly established investment board of federal officials and outside experts.

The system would be mandatory for all new workers. Current workers would have the option of joining the new system. Eventually, the individual accounts would provide for nearly all of Social Security's promised benefits.

When the worker reaches retirement age, he or she would either make phased withdrawals from the investment account or purchase an annuity, providing income for life. The worker's retirement income would be guaranteed and supplemented by Social Security if it does not produce benefits at least equal to benefits provided under the current Social Security System.

The payroll tax would gradually be reduced as the balances in the investment accounts build up over the years and provide for a greater share of promised benefits.

The transition to the new system would take place over fifty years. To help pay for the transitions—as payroll taxes are diverted into individual accounts—the government would use money from the growing federal budget surpluses.

REP. JOHN KASICH (R-OH) H.R. 3456

INDIVIDUAL ACCOUNTS: 80 percent of the federal budget surplus each year would be transferred to a new Social Security Plus Fund. The money would be allocated equally among all workers covered by Social Security.

The money would be distributed among investments similar to the Federal Thrift Savings Plan, which offers a choice among stocks, bonds, and Treasury bills.

There would be no taxes on the money contributed to the accounts. Any earnings also would be tax-free.

Individuals could withdraw the money when they begin drawing Social Security benefits. Withdrawals would be subject to normal income tax.

SEN. DANIEL PATRICK MOYNIHAN (D-NY)
SEN. J. ROBERT KERREY (D-NE) S.1792

PAYROLL TAXES: The payroll tax, now 12.4 percent of earnings up to $68,400 a year, would be reduced by one percentage point in 1999 and by an additional one percentage point in 2001, and then gradually increased to 13.8 percent by 2060.

INDIVIDUAL ACCOUNTS: Starting in 2001, a worker would have a choice: keep the 1.0 percentage point tax reduction as an increase in take-home pay, or place the money in a personal savings account. If the worker picks the savings account, the employer must match the 1.0 percentage point contribution.

The voluntary accounts could be administered for workers by the government or by private institutions. Funds in the accounts could be withdrawn only after the worker begins collecting Social Security benefits.

RETIREMENT AGE: The normal retirement age (for full benefits) would be increased in stages to age 70 by the year 2073.

COST-OF-LIVING ADJUSTMENT: The annual cost-of-living increase, which now matches the change in the Consumer Price Index (CPI), would be reduced by one percentage point. If the

CPI rises 3 percent, the increase in benefits would be 2 percent.

COMPUTATION YEARS: The number of years used for calculating retirement benefits, now thirty-five, would be increased to thirty-eight.

STATE AND LOCAL WORKERS: All newly hired state and local workers would be brought into the Social Security System, starting in 2001.

WAGE BASE: The maximum wage base on which taxes are paid would be raised to $96,600 by the year 2003. (Under current law, the figure is estimated to reach $82,800 in that year.)

REP. JERROLD NADLER (D-NY)

INVESTING THE TRUST FUNDS: Up to 50 percent of Social Security surpluses (in excess of a reserve equal to 100 percent of the annual payout) would be invested in private equities.

COST-OF-LIVING ADJUSTMENTS: Cost-of-living adjustments would reflect corrections to the Consumer Price Index (CPI) announced by the Bureau of Labor Statistics.

WAGE BASE: Under current law, the maximum wage base subject to payroll taxes would be 84.7 percent of earnings by 2007. The base would be increased, and then indexed, to 89 percent of earnings phased in from 1999 through 2009.

National Commission on Retirement Policy S.2313
SEN. JUDD GREGG (R-NH)
SEN. JOHN BREAUX (D-LA)
REP. JIM KOLBE (R-AZ)
REP. CHARLES STENHOLM (D-TX)

INDIVIDUAL ACCOUNTS: For all workers under age 55, the payroll tax would be cut by two percentage points, with the money going into personal accounts.

BENEFITS: The 32 percent and 15 percent bend point factors would be multiplied by 0.98 each year phased in from 2003 to 2022. A minimum benefits provision would be equal to 60 percent of the federal poverty line for those with twenty years of covered earnings. The base benefit would then increase by 2 percent a year until it reaches 100 percent of the poverty level for those with forty years of covered earnings. The minimum benefit would be payable if the amount exceeds benefits under the traditional benefit structure.

RETIREMENT AGE: Normal retirement age would be raised gradually to 70 by the year 2037. Age for early retirement benefits would be raised to age 65 by the year 2032. Ages would be increased thereafter by two months every three years, to keep pace with increased longevity. The delayed retirement credit (DRCs) and the actuarial adjustment for early retirement would be increased to allow workers to recover lost tax revenue for early/late retirement.

COMPUTATION YEARS: Number of working years for calculating benefits would be raised from thirty-five to forty, over a ten-year period starting in 2001. During this period, all years of earnings would be credited to the numerator of the Average Income Monthly Earnings (AIME).

STATE AND LOCAL WORKERS: All workers hired after 1999 would be covered by the Social Security System.

EARNINGS TEST: The current earnings test, which reduced benefits for those who work beyond retirement age, would be eliminated.

SPOUSAL BENEFIT: Aged spouses retirement benefit, now 50 percent of the worker's benefits, would be reduced to 33 percent, with the changes phased in between the years 2000 and 2016.

FAIL-SAFE MECHANISM: A mechanism is included to protect the program against variations in the long-term assumptions made by the Social Security Trustees.

REP. THOMAS E. PETRI (R-WI) H.R. 1611

INDIVIDUAL ACCOUNTS: Each person born on or after July 1, 1998 would have a Social Security investment account, with $1,000 deposited therein by the Treasury. The money would come from the sale of government assets.

The individual may contribute up to $7,000 each year to his or her own fund. Up to $2,000 of the annual contribution would be tax-deductible.

The money in the individual account could be invested in a selection of index funds similar to those offered by the Federal Thrift Savings Plan.

All the funds in the account would be used to pay the Social Security benefits earned by the worker. If the account has earned more than is needed to pay Social Security benefits, the worker would be allowed to receive the extra money in the form of an annuity.

REP. JOHN EDWARD PORTER (R-IL) H.R. 2929

INDIVIDUAL ACCOUNTS: Workers would be permitted to participate in a new voluntary private investment account. This would be an irrevocable choice. If they select the new account, 10 percent of the current 12.4 percent payroll tax would go into funding these new investments and the remaining 2.4 percent would go into the current system. Workers could make additional contributions of their own, with a limit of 20 percent of their gross income.

A portion of the investment fund would be used to buy private disability and life insurance policies equal to the protection now provided under Social Security.

Workers could withdraw the money from their individual accounts on retirement, starting at age 59½. The federal government would guarantee a minimum benefit for retirement. If the individuals account falls short, the government would make up the difference from general tax revenues.

RETIREMENT AGE: The full-benefits retirement age would be gradually increased and would be age 70 for workers born in 1967 or later.

BENEFIT SLOWDOWN: The formula for determining benefits would be reduced so that basic benefits rise with the increase in prices, rather than with the growth of wages in the economy each year. This would mean a slowdown in the size of benefits granted to new retirees.

SEN. WILLIAM V. ROTH, JR. (R-DE)

INDIVIDUAL ACCOUNTS: Each worker who earned at least the minimum needed for Social Security coverage ($2,880 for next year) would be eligible for an individual account deposit funded by the federal budget surplus. Half the surplus would be deposited in personal retirement accounts, with each American getting a minimum deposit of $250, plus an additional amount linked to the amount of payroll taxes paid by the wage earner.

The formula used for calculating the deposits would be progressive. For example, over five years of the program, a minimum wage earner would receive $1,724 deposited in his or her personal retirement account—equal to a 34 percent rebate of payroll taxes. Likewise, an average wage earner would receive $2,304 or a 20 percent rebate of his or her payroll taxes deposited in the account, and maximum earners would receive $3,842 or a 14 percent rebate of payroll taxes.

Account holders would have the choice between investing in a stock index fund, a corporate bond fund, or U.S. Treasury bonds.

When the individual reaches retirement age and applies for Social Security benefits, he or she could choose between purchasing an annuity or receiving payments through an installment plan.

REP. MARK SANFORD (R-SC) H.R. 2768

INDIVIDUAL ACCOUNTS: Workers entering the labor force in the year 2000 could contribute an amount equal to 4 percent of their earned income to a Personal Retirement Account (PRA). The employer would match an equal amount.

The money would be invested in a broad portfolio similar to an S&P 500 mutual fund. The money would build up until there is enough to purchase an annuity yielding an income of $840 a month (indexed for inflation). This would be a guaranteed minimum benefit. If the PRA is not large enough to purchase this annuity, the difference would be made up by the government.

There is also a FDIC-type of insurance against failure of a custodian or massive market downturn close to the time of retirement.

Any funds that build up beyond the amount needed to generate $840 a month could be invested in any asset selected by the worker. These extra funds would be uninsured.

Current workers can also choose to switch to the new individual accounts. They would get a pension equal to the Social Security benefits which they had already earned.

RETIREMENT AGE: The full-benefits retirement age would be gradually increased to age 70 by the year 2029.

SPOUSAL BENEFIT: The spousal benefit for aged workers would be decreased from 50 percent of the workers benefit to 33 percent.

STATE AND LOCAL WORKERS: All new state and local workers would be covered by Social Security.

REP. PETE SESSIONS (R-TX) H.R. 3683

INDIVIDUAL ACCOUNTS: Any worker could choose to opt out of Social Security by having his, or her, taxes of 6.2 percent directed into a personal account. It could be invested in anything qualified for Individual Retirement Accounts (IRA), such as stocks, bonds, money market accounts and mutual funds.

The employer would continue to match the worker's 6.2 percent contribution for fifteen years. The money would be deposited into the worker's personal account in the sixteenth year.

A worker who chooses to leave the system would have dual coverage for ninety days under Social Security and the new program, called Savings Accounts for every American (SAFE). Social Security coverage would decline by 20 percent each year and the worker would give up Social Security eligibility entirely at the end of the fifth year.

Workers can spend money tax free from the SAFE account to buy personal disability and life insurance coverage.

REP. NICK SMITH (R-MI) H.R. 3082

INDIVIDUAL ACCOUNTS: Each worker could contribute a portion of payroll taxes into a Personal Retirement Savings Account

(PRSA). The contribution would start at 2.5 percent of covered wages in 1999 and rise to 10.2 percent over seventy-five years.

The amount accumulated in the personal account would be used to buy an annuity when the worker reaches retirement age.

The amount of Social Security retirement benefits would be reduced as the value of the personal account increases. Social Security benefits would be virtually eliminated by the year 2067, and replaced by the personal account.

RETIREMENT AGE: The full-benefits retirement age would be gradually increased, reaching age 69 in approximately the year 2022, and then would keep rising about one month every two years as life expectancy rises. The age for receiving early retirement benefits would be increased gradually reaching age 65 in the year 2014.

COMPUTATION YEARS: The number of years used in calculating Social Security retirement benefits would be increased from thirty-five to thirty-nine by the year 2018.

SPOUSAL BENEFIT: The aged spouses retirement benefit, now equal to 50 percent of a workers retirement benefit, would be reduced to 33⅓ percent. The change would be phased in between 2000 and 2016.

The widow's and widower's benefit, now 100 percent of the workers benefit, would be raised to 110 percent after 1998.

STATE AND LOCAL WORKERS: Newly hired state and local workers would be covered by the Social Security System.

Notes

Chapter 1

1. *The Coming Collapse of Social Security* (Madison, VA: TREA Senior Citizens League, 1995).
2. Leon F. Bouvier, "America's Baby Boom Generation: The Fateful Bulge," *Population Bulletin* (April 1980): 4.
3. Ibid., p. 5.
4. *Economic Report of the President* (Washington, DC: United States Government Printing Office, 1997), p. 337.
5. Bouvier, "America's Baby Boom Generation," p. 18.
6. Ibid., p. 6.
7. Paul C. Light, *Baby Boomers* (New York: W.W. Norton, 1988), p. 24.
8. *Statistical Abstract of the United States: 1994* (Washington, DC: United States Government Printing Office, 1994), p. 78.
9. Bouvier, "America's Baby Boom Generation," p. 21; *Statistical Abstract,* p. 177.
10. *Statistical Abstract,* pp. 136, 177.
11. Ibid., p. 58; *Economic Report of the President,* p. 361.
12. *Statistical Abstract,* p. 58.
13. *Economic Report of the President,* p. 338.
14. Bouvier, "America's Baby Boom Generation," p. 29; *Economic Report of the President,* p. 338.
15. *Economic Report of the President,* p. 337; *Statistical Abstract,* p. 14.
16. Virginia P. Reno and Robert B. Friedland, "Strong Support but Low Confidence: What Explains the Contradiction?" in *Social Security in the 21st Century,* Eric R. Kingson and James H. Schulz, eds. (New York, Oxford University Press, 1997), pp. 178–194.
17. *Economic Report of the President,* p. 391.
18. Ibid., pp. 300, 391.
19. *Current Economic Indicators* (Washington, DC: United States Government Printing Office, April 1998), pp. 1, 34.
20. A. Haeworth Robertson, *Social Security: What Every Taxpayer Should Know* (Washington, DC: Retirement Policy Institute, 1992), p. 154.
21. Board of Trustees, Federal Supplementary Medical Insurance Trust

Fund, *The 1997 Annual Report of the Board of Trustees of the Federal Supplementary Medical Insurance Trust Fund* (Washington, DC: United States Government Printing Office, 1997), pp. 29, 55.

22. Board of Trustees, Federal Old Age and Survivors Insurance and Disability Insurance Trust Funds, *The 1997 Annual Report of the Board of Trustees of the Federal Old-Age and Survivors Insurance and Disability Insurance Trust Funds* (Washington, DC: United States Government Printing Office, 1997), p. 148.

Chapter 2

1. George E. Rejda, *Social Insurance and Economic Security*, 3rd ed. (Englewood Cliffs, NJ: Prentice Hall, 1988), pp. 32–33.
2. Harrell R. Rodgers, Jr., *The Cost of Human Neglect* (New York: M.E. Sharpe, 1982), p. 52.
3. Edward D. Berkowitz, "The Historical Development of Social Security in the United States," in *Social Security in the 21st Century,* Eric R. Kingson and James H. Schulz, eds. (New York: Oxford University Press, 1997), p. 28.
4. *Economic Report of the President,* (Washington, DC: United States Government Printing Office, 1997), p. 352, 1967 edition, p. 248.
5. Berkowitz, "The Historical Development of Social Security," p. 31.
6. Committee on Ways and Means, U.S. House of Representatives, *Overview of the Federal Tax System* (Washington, DC: United States Government Printing Office, 1991), p. 179.
7. Board of Trustees, Federal Supplementary Medical Insurance Trust Fund, *The 1997 Annual Report of the Board of Trustees of the Federal Supplementary Medical Insurance Trust Fund* (Washington, DC: United States Government Printing Office, 1997), p. 4.
8. Ibid., p. 22.
9. Rejda, *Social Insurance,* p. 220.
10. Ibid., p. 221.
11. Ibid., p. 362.
12. Social Security Administration, *Annual Statistical Supplement to the Social Security Bulletin* (Washington, DC: United States Government Printing Office, 1995), p. 176. The money borrowed was repaid in 1985 and 1986.
13. *Report of the National Commission on Social Security Reform* (Washington, DC: United States Government Printing Office, 1993), Ch. 2, p. 2.
14. *Annual Statistical Supplement to the Social Security Bulletin,* p. 176.
15. Ibid.
16. Board of Trustees, p. 182.
17. Rejda, *Social Insurance,* p. 67.
18. Board of Trustees, p. 63.
19. Paul C. Light, *Baby Boomers* (New York: W.W. Norton, 1988), p. 277.
20. Board of Trustees, p. 148.
21. Ibid., p. 63.

22. Quoted in Light, *Baby Boomers,* p. 276.
23. *Economic Report of the President*, pp. 350–351.
24. Elliot Carlson, Interview with Alvin Toffler in *AARP Bulletin,* December 1995, p. 16.

Chapter 3

1. See Table 1.5
2. *Newsletter,* United Seniors Association, Inc., (USA), July 1998.
3. Ibid.
4. Peter G. Peterson, *Will America Grow Up Before It Grows Old?* (New York: Random House, 1996), p. 47.
5. The Board of Trustees, Federal Old Age and Survivors Insurance and Disability Insurance Trust Funds, *1997 Annual Report of the Board of Trustees of the Federal Old-Age and Survivors Insurance and Disability Insurance Trust Funds.* (Washington, DC: U.S. Government Printing Office, 1997), pp. 213, 217.
6. Ibid., pp. 106–107.
7. *Newsletter,* USA, Inc.
8. *Newsletter,* USA, Inc., computerized letter to Senator Trent Lott, United States Senate.
9. Joint Economic Committee. *Economic Indicators,* June 1998. (Washington, DC: U.S. Government Printing Office, June 1998), p. 32.
10. Board of Trustees, p. 11.
11. Ibid., p. 26.
12. There is no upper limit on wages and salaries subject to the payroll tax for hospital insurance (HI).
13. Board of Trustees, pp. 175, 190; *Economic Indicators,* pp. 1, 33.
14. See Table A 3.1. Social Security Administration, *Understanding the Benefits* (Washington, DC: Social Security Administration, 1998), p. 36.
15. Social Security Administration, *Annual Statistical Supplement, Social Security Bulletin* (Washington, DC: U.S. Government Printing Office, 1995), pp. 196–205.
16. Ibid.
17. Ibid.
18. Testimony of Shirley Chater, U.S. Commissioner of Social Security, before Senate Finance Committee, U.S. Congress, *Hearing on Social Security and the Future of Retirees,* 104th Congress, 2nd Session, March 11, 1996.
19. In 1996, a special congressional committee of economists reported that the CPI was biased on the high side by about 1.2 percentage points per year. If the CPI were adjusted to reflect this criticism, it would mean a de facto reduction in annual increases in Social Security benefits. To date, no changes have been made in the CPI.
20. U.S. Department of Commerce, Bureau of the Census, *Current Population Reports,* Series P60–186RD, *Measuring the Effect of Benefits and Taxes*

on Income and Poverty: 1992 (Washington, DC: U.S. Government Printing Office, 1993).

21. Ibid., p. xii.

22. Ibid.

23. For an explanation of poverty and its measurement, see pp. A-1 ff. in *Current Population Reports,* Series P60–186RD.

24. *Current Population Reports,* Series P60–186RD, p. xxiii.

25. Ibid., p. xxii.

26. TREA Senior Citizens League, *The Coming Collapse of Social Security,* (Madison, VA: The Senior Exchange, 1995), pp. 15 ff.

27. Ibid., p. 18. (Italics added.)

28. Ibid., p. 19.

Chapter 4

1. Because of the Roman Catholic Church, Copernicus's theory was not published until after his death.

2. Board of Trustees, Federal Old-Age and Survivors Insurance and Disability Insurance Trust Funds, *1997 Annual Report* (Washington, DC: U.S. Government Printing Office, 1997), p. 148.

3. Calculated from *1997 Annual Report,* p. 124, and *Economic Report of the President,* 1997, p. 338.

4. Ibid.

5. Calculated from Table 4.3.

6. The earned income tax credit provides cash income to families whose income falls below a designated level. It is a limited form of the negative income tax proposed by Milton Friedman.

7. *Current Economic Indicators,* July 1998, p. 1.

8. U.S. Bureau of the Census, *Current Population Reports* P60–185RD, 1993.

9. *Bipartisan Commission on Entitlements and Tax Reform,* (Washington, DC: Superintendent of Documents, 1995). Referred to henceforth as the Kerrey-Danforth Report.

10. Kerrey-Danforth Report, p. 9.

11. Ibid., pp. 155–169.

12. Committee on the Budget, United States Senate, *Tax Expenditures: Relationships to Spending Programs and Background Material on Individual Provisions* (Washington, DC: U.S. Government Printing Office, 1982), p. 1

13. Kerrey-Danforth Report, pp. 85–89.

14. Ibid., pp. 49–51.

15. Herman B. Leonard, *Checks Unbalanced: The Quiet Side of Public Spending* (New York: Basic Books, 1986), p. 28.

16. Ibid., p. 60.

17. Ibid., p. 61.

18. Peter G. Peterson, *Will America Grow Up Before It Grows Old? How*

the Coming Social Security Crisis Threatens You, Your Family, and Your Country (New York: Random House, 1996), p. 44.

19. Ibid., p. 47.
20. Ibid.
21. Board of Trustees, p. 71.
22. See discussion in Chapter 3.

Chapter 5

1. The Board of Trustees, Federal Old-Age and Survivors Insurance and Disability Insurance Trust Funds, *1998 Annual Report of the Board of Trustees of the Federal Old-Age and Survivors Insurance and Disability Trust Funds* (Washington, DC: U.S. Government Printing Office, 1998), p. 179.
2. *Economic Report of the President* (Washington, DC: U.S. Government Printing Office, 1997), pp. 300, 401, 406.
3. United States Senate, S. 1792, "Social Security Solvency Act of 1998."
4. The Social Security Advisory Board is appointed jointly by the President and Congress. The most recent report of the Board was issued in 1996.
5. Walter M. Cadette, "Social Security: The Challenge of Financing the Baby-Boom's Retirement," Working Paper No. 192, The Jerome Levy Economics Institute, April 1997, p. 21.
6. Calculation by author.
7. Ibid.; *Economic Report of the President,* pp. 365, 405.
8. *U.S. News and World Report,* May 11, 1998.
9. *U.S.A. Today,* January 18, 1997.
10. John Mueller, *Challenge,* "The Stock Market Won't Beat Social Security," vol. 41, no. 2, March–April 1998, p. 95.
11. Ibid.
12. The administrative costs are estimated to be as high as 20 percent.
13. Council of Economic Advisers, *Current Economic Indicators,* August 1998, p. 6; *Economic Report of the President,* p. 322.
14. *Economic Report of the President,* Ibid., pp. 300, 334.
15. Ibid., pp. 300, 301.
16. Frederick R. Strobel and Wallace C. Peterson, *The Coming Class War and How to Avoid It,* (Armonk, NY: M.E. Sharpe, 1999), p. 119.
17. Ibid., p. 121.
18. Board of Trustees, p. 173.
19. Ibid., p. 120.
20. Ibid., p. 23.
21. The Board of Trustees, Federal Hospital Insurance Fund, *1998 Annual Report of the Board of Trustees of the Federal Hospital Insurance Trust Fund* (Washington, DC: U.S. Government Printing Office, 1998), p. 77.
22. Americans Discuss Social Security, 2001 Pennsylvania Avenue, NW, Suite 825, Washington, D.C. 2006.

23. Robert Eisner, "Save Social Security From its Saviors," *Journal of Post Keynesian Economics* 21, No. 1 (fall 1988): 78.

24. Ibid.

25. Peter G. Peterson, *Will America Grow Up Before It Grows Old?* (New York: Random House, 1996), p. 162.

26. *Economic Report of the President,* p. 395; *Current Economic Indicators,* August 1998, p. 34.

27. *Current Economic Indicators,* ibid., p. 4; *1998 Annual Report of the Board of Trustees of the Federal Old-Age and Survivors Insurance Trust Fund and Disability Insurance Trust Fund,* p. 175.

28. Congress of the United States, Joint Economic Committee, *Staff Report on Employment, Growth and Taxes* (Washington, DC: U.S. Government Printing Office, 1959).

29. Wallace C. Peterson. *Income, Employment, and Economic Growth,* 8th ed. (New York: W.W. Norton, 1996), p. 550.

30. Ibid.

31. Ibid.

32. *1998 Annual Report,* Board of Trustees, p. 57.

33. Ibid.

34. *Economic Report of the President,* pp. 300, 328.

35. *1998 Annual Report,* Board of Trustees, p. 119. The 13.369 rate does not include the Medicare payroll tax.

36. Wallace C. Peterson, *Silent Depression: The Fate of the American Dream* (New York: W.W. Norton, 1994).

37. Computed by author.

38. *Economic Report of the President,* pp. 337–338.

39. Paul Krugman, *The Age of Diminished Expectations* (Cambridge: MIT Press, 1990), p. 9.

40. *Current Economic Indicators,* February 1999, p. 16.

41. The phrase, "Military Keynesianism," was coined by the British economist, the late Joan Robinson, in an address to American economists in 1971. She used the phrase to describe how high-level military expenditures had become a major force in the American economy during the Cold War years.

42. "Infrastructure" consists of public capital such a streets and highways, water and sewer systems, educational buildings, hospitals, and other tools and structures constructed and used by public bodies.

43. See David Alan Aschauer, "How Big Should the Public Capital Stock Be?" *Public Policy Brief,* The Jerome Levy Economics Institute, Barnard College, September 1998.

44. Peterson, *Silent Depression,* p. 200.

45. *Current Economic Indicators,* August 1998, p. 34.

46. Aschauer, *Back of the G-7 Pack: Public Investment and Productivity Growth in the Group of Seven* (Chicago: Federal Reserve Bank of Chicago, 1989).

Index

C

D

E

T

U

V

W

Y

Z

Wallace C. Peterson completed his education at the University of Nebraska, getting his BA, MA, and Ph.D. in 1947, 1948, and 1953, respectively. His professional career has been at NU, where he has been the George Holmes Professor of Economics since 1966, and served as the Chairman of the Department of Economics from 1965–75. He has written eight books, several monographs, and over 50 scholarly articles. He is a past President of the Midwest Economics Association, the Association for Evolutionary Economics, the Association of Social Economics, and the Missouri Valley Economics Association. In addition, he was Editor of the *Nebraska Journal of Economics and Business* from 1974–1982.